CAMBRIDGE LATIN GRAMMAR

R. M. GRIFFIN

CAMBRIDGE
UNIVERSITY PRESS

PUBLISHED BY THE PRESS SYNDICATE OF THE UNIVERSITY OF CAMBRIDGE
The Pitt Building, Trumpington Street, Cambridge CB2 1RP, United Kingdom

CAMBRIDGE UNIVERSITY PRESS
The Edinburgh Building, Cambridge CB2 2RU, United Kingdom
40 West 20th Street, New York, NY 10011–4211, USA
10 Stamford Road, Oakleigh, Melbourne 3166, Australia

First published 1991
Sixth printing 1997

Printed in the United Kingdom at the University Press, Cambridge

A catalogue record for this book is available from the British Library

ISBN 0 521 38588 1 paperback

Text design by Marcus Askwith

Cover picture: wall painting from Pompeii showing Paquius Proculus and his
wife; reproduced by courtesy of The Ancient Art and Architecture Collection.

ACKNOWLEDGEMENTS

I should like to express my warmest thanks to the many people who have helped with the writing and production of this grammar: the members of the Cambridge School Classics Project team; the Cambridge University Press editorial staff; Professor Allen and Cambridge University Press for permission to make use of the summary of recommended pronunciation in *Vox Latina* by W.S. Allen (C.U.P. 1965, 2nd edition 1978); and many others who have scrutinised draft material, made suggestions and criticisms, and been ever-ready with advice, encouragement and support. I should in particular like to thank Patricia Acres, Maire Collins, William Duggan, Vivienne Hayward, Jean Hubbard, Professor E.J. Kenney, Anne Mathews, Elizabeth Merrylees, Martin Moore, Betty Munday, Nick Munday, Pam Perkins, Professor Ed Phinney, Keith Rose, Tim Scragg, Pat Story, Alex Sutherland and David Wilson. I have gratefully adopted many of the suggestions made by those who read the grammar at draft stage; responsibility for errors and omissions is mine.

R.M. Griffin
Cambridge School Classics Project

CONTENTS

STUDENT'S INTRODUCTION

This book is designed for two purposes:

1 *Reference*, i.e. for looking up a point that is causing difficulty or uncertainty. Part One ('Accidence') sets out the full system of Latin word-endings, and should be consulted if you come across an ending which you cannot confidently identify. Part Two ('Syntax') describes the chief ways in which the various word-endings are used, and should be consulted if you are unsure how a word fits into a particular sentence. Parts Three and Four cover a mixture of other points, and are mostly concerned with revision rather than reference (but Section **32**, 'How to use a Latin–English dictionary', and Section **33**, on the subjunctive, may sometimes be useful in cases of difficulty).

   If you know the *name* for the Latin word or phrase which is giving trouble (e.g. if you know that it is an adjective but are not sure about its case, or if you know that it is a conditional clause or indirect statement but are uncertain about its translation), the quickest way to find the information you need is by using the index on pages 120–7.

2 *Revision*, i.e. for practising a particular point (e.g. the formation of participles, the various uses of the ablative case, the different sorts of subordinate clause, the details of indirect speech, or the ways in which the Romans expressed ideas of time and place). After studying the relevant section or paragraph, you may find it helpful to work through any exercise or 'further examples' included in the section; these will often make it clear to you whether you have understood the point.

The numbers of *sections* are printed in bold type; the numbers of *paragraphs* are printed in ordinary type. All cross-references from one section to another give the numbers of the section and the relevant paragraph(s); for example '**11**.7' refers to Section **11**, paragraph 7, and '**20**.1–4' refers to Section **20**, paragraphs 1–4.

TEACHER'S INTRODUCTION

The Cambridge Latin Grammar is designed for reference and revision, as described above in the Student's Introduction. Teachers may wish not only to encourage students to use it for reference and private study, but also to take the class through selected sections for oral work. It will often be helpful to link study of the grammar with work on the Latin text currently being read in class.

The book is intended for use by anyone who needs a Latin grammar at a level midway between elementary and advanced, but it has been devised with two particular groups of users in mind: students in the final year of a GCSE course, who have passed from the stage of 'made-up' Latin to reading wholly or mainly unadapted texts of original Roman authors, and post-GCSE students who have just started a sixth-form Latin course and wish to revise and consolidate before making the transition to a more advanced reference grammar. Both groups of users, it is hoped, will find that this grammar provides them with a convenient basis for revision and helps with some of the difficulties which may arise during the reading of their Latin texts.

The grammar takes its basic plan, and some of its material, from the Language Information sections of the Cambridge Latin Course but is deliberately designed to be equally accessible to users of other courses. Its contents have been drawn up with an eye to the grammatical requirements of current GCSE syllabuses, though it probably covers a wider range of linguistic features than any one syllabus. It includes all the features discussed in the Cambridge Latin Course's language notes and Language Information sections, together with some points which occur in the Course's reading material without being explicitly discussed (e.g. causal and concessive clauses) and one or two further points which do not appear in the Course at all (e.g. *quō* with the subjunctive). Teachers who have taken their students through the Course but been forced by time shortage to cut down on their coverage of grammatical points will find (provided that their omissions have not been too extensive) that this grammar offers a chance to fill in some of the gaps. Those who wish to add comment on features which have not been included (e.g. *quīn*) may like to make use of the blank pages which have been provided at the end of the book for additional notes by the students.

Some linguistic points are deliberately covered from more than one point of view; for example *nōlī* with the infinitive appears in its appropriate place in Section **12** ('Commands'), but reappears briefly in

Section **21**, which gathers together the various uses of the infinitive in summary form for study and comparison. Some material which strictly belongs more to a vocabulary-list than to a grammar (e.g. lists of common prepositions, verbs governing the dative, principal parts of common verbs, etc.) has been included for the student's convenience. A section towards the end gives guidance on, and practice in, the use of a Latin–English dictionary. Small type (sometimes accompanied by a vertical bar in the margin) has been used not only for cross-references and footnotes but also as a rough indication of points which may be regarded as more peripheral, or more advanced, than the rest; but teachers will wish to exercise their own judgement over whether, and how far, to explore a given point with their students. As the grammar is not designed for use by advanced learners, its treatment of the language is necessarily selective and at times over-simplified; but it is hoped that it will not be found to be seriously misleading.

Most of the linguistic features covered in this grammar (especially from Part Two onwards) are illustrated by a number of translated examples; many students find that they grasp a point more quickly and securely by studying examples than by reading a description. Also included are several exercises (mainly in Part One, e.g. Sections **1**, **2**, **5** and **7**) and a large number of untranslated 'further examples' (especially in Parts Two, Three and Four) designed to give the student practice in the various points covered. The vocabulary used in the examples is mainly but not wholly restricted to words which occur in the checklists of the Cambridge Latin Course.

The book is primarily designed for students whose aim is to read and understand a Latin text and translate it into English when required. This does not mean that such points as 3rd-declension genitive plurals and the rule of 'sequence of tenses', which assume extra importance for the student whose aim is to translate *into* Latin, have been omitted; but teachers whose special concern is with English-into-Latin composition may find it necessary to amplify the book's exposition of these points with further comment of their own (for which, again, the blank pages at the end may be useful).

PART ONE

ACCIDENCE
(word-endings)

1 Nouns

1 *first declension*
puella, f.* 'girl':

	SINGULAR	PLURAL
nominative and vocative	puell**a**	puell**ae**
accusative	puell**am**	puell**ās**
genitive	puell**ae**	puell**ārum**
dative	puell**ae**	puell**īs**
ablative	puell**ā**	puell**īs**

2 *second declension*
servus, m.* 'slave'; **puer**, m. 'boy'; **magister**, m. 'teacher'; **templum**, n.* 'temple':

SINGULAR				
nominative and vocative	serv**us** (*voc.* serv**e**)	puer	magister	templ**um**
accusative	serv**um**	puer**um**	magistr**um**	templ**um**
genitive	serv**ī**	puer**ī**	magistr**ī**	templ**ī**
dative	serv**ō**	puer**ō**	magistr**ō**	templ**ō**
ablative	serv**ō**	puer**ō**	magistr**ō**	templ**ō**
PLURAL				
nominative and vocative	serv**ī**	puer**ī**	magistr**ī**	templ**a**
accusative	serv**ōs**	puer**ōs**	magistr**ōs**	templ**a**
genitive	serv**ōrum**	puer**ōrum**	magistr**ōrum**	templ**ōrum**
dative	serv**īs**	puer**īs**	magistr**īs**	templ**īs**
ablative	serv**īs**	puer**īs**	magistr**īs**	templ**īs**

Some 2nd-declension nouns whose nominative and vocative singular ends in -*er*, e.g. *gener*, form their endings in the same way as *puer*; others, e.g. *ager*, form their endings like *magister*.

2nd-declension nouns whose nominative singular ends in -*ius* (e.g. *fīlius*) have a vocative singular ending in -*ī* (e.g. *fīlī*).

2nd-declension nouns whose nominative singular ends in -*ius* or -*ium* (e.g. *fīlius, cōnsilium*) sometimes shorten the ending of their genitive singular from -*iī* to -*ī* (e.g. *fīlī* instead of *fīliī*, and *cōnsilī* instead of *cōnsiliī*).

* f. = feminine; m. = masculine; n. = neuter.

deus, m. 'god' and *vir*, m. 'man' have the following forms:

	SINGULAR	PLURAL	SINGULAR	PLURAL
nominative and vocative	deus	deī/dī	vir	virī
accusative	deum	deōs	virum	virōs
genitive	deī	deōrum/deum	virī	virōrum/virum
dative	deō	deīs/dīs	virō	virīs
ablative	deō	deīs/dīs	virō	virīs

3 *third declension*
mercātor, m. 'merchant'; **leō**, m. 'lion'; **cīvis**, m. 'citizen'; **rēx**, m. 'king'; **urbs**, f. 'city'; **nōmen**, n. 'name'; **tempus**, n. 'time'; **mare**, n. 'sea':

SINGULAR

nom. and voc.	mercātor	leō	cīvis	rēx	urbs	nōmen	tempus	mare
acc.	mercātōrem	leōnem	cīvem	rēgem	urbem	nōmen	tempus	mare
gen.	mercātōris	leōnis	cīvis	rēgis	urbis	nōminis	temporis	maris
dat.	mercātōrī	leōnī	cīvī	rēgī	urbī	nōminī	temporī	marī
abl.	mercātōre	leōne	cīve	rēge	urbe	nōmine	tempore	marī

PLURAL

nom. and voc.	mercātōrēs	leōnēs	cīvēs	rēgēs	urbēs	nōmina	tempora	maria
acc.	mercātōrēs	leōnēs	cīvēs	rēgēs	urbēs	nōmina	tempora	maria
gen.	mercātōrum	leōnum	cīvium	rēgum	urbium	nōminum	temporum	marium
dat.	mercātōribus	leōnibus	cīvibus	rēgibus	urbibus	nōminibus	temporibus	maribus
abl.	mercātōribus	leōnibus	cīvibus	rēgibus	urbibus	nōminibus	temporibus	maribus

3rd-declension nouns form their genitive plural in the following ways:
(i) nouns whose genitive singular contains more syllables than their nominative singular (e.g. *leō*, genitive *leōnis*) have a genitive plural ending in *-um* (e.g. *leōnum*).
Exceptions: nouns whose nominative singular contains only one syllable and which have two consonants before the *-is* of their genitive singular (e.g. *mōns*, genitive *montis*) have a genitive plural ending in *-ium* (e.g. *montium*).
(ii) nouns whose genitive singular has the same number of syllables as their nominative singular (e.g. *cīvis*, genitive *cīvis*) have a genitive plural ending in *-ium* (e.g. *cīvium*).
Exceptions: *pater*, *māter*, *frāter*, *senex*, *iuvenis* and *canis* have a genitive plural ending in *-um* (e.g. *patrum*).

3rd-declension neuter nouns whose nominative singular ends in *-e*, *-al* or *-ar* (e.g. *conclāve*, *animal*) change their endings in the same way as *mare*. Their ablative singular ends in *-ī* (e.g. *conclāvī*, *animālī*) and their genitive plural ends in *-ium* (e.g. *conclāvium*, *animālium*).

4   *fourth declension*
manus, f. 'hand' and **genū**, n. 'knee':

	SINGULAR	PLURAL	SINGULAR	PLURAL
nominative and vocative	man**us**	man**ūs**	gen**ū**	gen**ua**
accusative	man**um**	man**ūs**	gen**ū**	gen**ua**
genitive	man**ūs**	man**uum**	gen**ūs**	gen**uum**
dative	man**uī**	man**ibus**	gen**ū**	gen**ibus**
ablative	man**ū**	man**ibus**	gen**ū**	gen**ibus**

The irregular noun *domus*, f. 'house, home' has the following forms:

	SINGULAR	PLURAL
nominative and vocative	dom**us**	dom**ūs**
accusative	dom**um**	dom**ūs**/dom**ōs**
genitive	dom**ūs**	dom**uum**/dom**ōrum**
dative	dom**uī**	dom**ibus**
ablative	dom**ō**	dom**ibus**

5   *fifth declension*
diēs, m. 'day':

	SINGULAR	PLURAL
nominative and vocative	di**ēs**	di**ēs**
accusative	di**em**	di**ēs**
genitive	di**ēī**	di**ērum**
dative	di**ēī**	di**ēbus**
ablative	di**ē**	di**ēbus**

6   For examples of ways in which the different cases are used, see **14**.1–6.

7   With the help of paragraphs 1–5, and of **14**.1–6, work out the Latin for the italicised words:

   1   We soon entered the *city*.
   2   The governor provided a ship for the *merchants*.
   3   The mother of the *girl* lived nearby.
   4   The visitor was admiring the *temples*.
   5   Come here, *slave*!
   6   The *lions* were lying under a tree.
   7   It was now the third hour of the *day*.
   8   I handed the *boy* a wax tablet.
   9   An attendant read out the *citizens'* names.
   10 This letter was written by the *hand* of the *king* himself.

8   Sometimes the plural of a noun is used with a singular meaning, especially in verse:

per amīca **silentia** lūnae
through the friendly silence of the moonlight

9   The gender of a Latin noun depends

(i) partly on its meaning:
nouns referring to males   – masculine
nouns referring to females – feminine
nouns referring to things   – masculine, feminine or neuter

(ii) partly on its declension:
most 1st- and 5th-declension nouns   – feminine
most 2nd- and 4th-declension nouns ending in -*us* – masculine
all 2nd-declension nouns ending in -*um* }
and 4th-declension nouns ending in -*ū* }   – neuter

(iii) partly on the ending of the nominative singular. For example:
most 3rd-declension nouns ending in -*or*   – masculine
many 3rd-declension nouns ending in -*is*   – feminine
However, the ending of the nominative singular is only a rough guide to the gender of a noun, and cannot be relied on as a fixed rule.

10   Some place-names have a *locative* case, formed in the following ways:

	nominative	locative
1st-declension: singular	Rōma ('Rome')	Rōmae ('at Rome')
plural	Athēnae ('Athens')	Athēnīs ('at Athens')
2nd-declension: singular	Eboracum ('York')	Eboracī ('at York')
plural	Philippī ('Philippi')	Philippīs ('at Philippi')
3rd-declension: singular	Neapolis ('Naples')	Neapolī/Neapole ('at Naples')
plural	Gādēs ('Cadiz')	Gādibus ('at Cadiz')

The nouns *domus*, *humus* and *rūs* have locatives *domī* 'at home', *humī* 'on the ground' and *rūrī* 'in the countryside'.

For examples of the way the locative case is used, see **15**.2d(iii).

2 Adjectives

1 *first and second declension*
   bonus 'good'; **pulcher** 'beautiful'; **miser** 'unhappy':

	masculine	feminine	neuter	masculine	feminine	neuter
SINGULAR						
nominative and vocative	**bonus** (*voc.* bone)	bona	bon**um**	pulcher	pulchra	pulchr**um**
accusative	bon**um**	bon**am**	bon**um**	pulchr**um**	pulchr**am**	pulchr**um**
genitive	bon**ī**	bon**ae**	bon**ī**	pulchr**ī**	pulchr**ae**	pulchr**ī**
dative	bon**ō**	bon**ae**	bon**ō**	pulchr**ō**	pulchr**ae**	pulchr**ō**
ablative	bon**ō**	bon**ā**	bon**ō**	pulchr**ō**	pulchr**ā**	pulchr**ō**
PLURAL						
nominative and vocative	bon**ī**	bon**ae**	bona	pulchr**ī**	pulchr**ae**	pulchra
accusative	bon**ōs**	bon**ās**	bona	pulchr**ōs**	pulchr**ās**	pulchra
genitive	bon**ōrum**	bon**ārum**	bon**ōrum**	pulchr**ōrum**	pulchr**ārum**	pulchr**ōrum**
dative		bon**īs**			pulchr**īs**	
ablative		bon**īs**			pulchr**īs**	

	masculine	feminine	neuter
SINGULAR			
nominative and vocative	miser	misera	miser**um**
accusative	miser**um**	miser**am**	miser**um**
genitive	miser**ī**	miser**ae**	miser**ī**
dative	miser**ō**	miser**ae**	miser**ō**
ablative	miser**ō**	miser**ā**	miser**ō**
PLURAL			
nominative and vocative	miser**ī**	miser**ae**	misera
accusative	miser**ōs**	miser**ās**	misera
genitive	miser**ōrum**	miser**ārum**	miser**ōrum**
dative		miser**īs**	
ablative		miser**īs**	

2   *third declension*
ācer 'keen, sharp'; **fortis** 'brave'; **fēlīx** 'fortunate'; **ingēns** 'huge'; **vetus** 'old':

	masculine	*feminine*	*neuter*	*masc. and fem.*	*neuter*	*masc. and fem.*	*neuter*
SINGULAR							
nominative and vocative	ācer	ācris	ācre	fortis	forte	fēlīx	fēlīx
accusative	ācrem	ācrem	ācre	fortem	forte	fēlīcem	fēlīx
genitive		ācris			fortis		fēlīcis
dative		ācrī			fortī		fēlīcī
ablative		ācrī			fortī		fēlīcī
PLURAL							
nominative and vocative	ācrēs	ācrēs	ācria	fortēs	fortia	fēlīcēs	fēlīcia
accusative	ācrēs	ācrēs	ācria	fortēs	fortia	fēlīcēs	fēlīcia
genitive		ācrium			fortium		fēlīcium
dative		ācribus			fortibus		fēlīcibus
ablative		ācribus			fortibus		fēlīcibus

	masc. and fem.	*neuter*	*masc. and fem.*	*neuter*
SINGULAR				
nominative and vocative	ingēns	ingēns	vetus	vetus
accusative	ingentem	ingēns	veterem	vetus
genitive	ingentis		veteris	
dative	ingentī		veterī	
ablative	ingentī		vetere	
PLURAL				
nominative and vocative	ingentēs	ingentia	veterēs	vetera
accusative	ingentēs	ingentia	veterēs	vetera
genitive	ingentium		veterum	
dative	ingentibus		veteribus	
ablative	ingentibus		veteribus	

A few adjectives (e.g. *dīves, pauper*) change their endings in the same way as *vetus*. Their ablative singular ends in *-e* (e.g. *dīvite, paupere*) and their genitive plural ends in *-um* (e.g. *dīvitum, pauperum*).

For an example of the way in which *comparative* adjectives change their endings, see *lātior* in **4**.1.

3   For examples of agreement between adjectives and nouns, see **17**.2.

4   For examples of adjectives used attributively and predicatively, see **18**.1–7.

5   For examples of various types of word order involving nouns and adjectives, see **29**.1–7.

6   *Exercise*   With the help of **1**.1–5, paragraphs 1 and 2 above and **14**.1–6, work out the Latin for the italicised words:

1 I gave a reward to the *brave citizen*.
2 The visitors admired the *beautiful temples*.
3 The *unhappy merchants* returned home.
4 We listened to the words of the *fortunate boy*.
5 They were startled by a *huge shout*.
   (*clāmor* changes its endings in the same way as *mercātor*.)
6 The deeds of *good kings* are never forgotten.

7   Masculine, feminine and neuter forms of adjectives can be used on their own (i.e. unaccompanied by nouns) with the meanings '. . . man, men', '. . . woman, women' and '. . . thing, things':

bonus	a good man	nostrī	our men
multae	many women	vēra	true things
omnia	all things, everything		(i.e. 'the truth')

3 Adverbs

Formed from adjectives in the following ways:

adjective	*adverb*
first and second declension	
lātus *wide* (*genitive* lātī)	lātē *widely*
pulcher *beautiful* (*gen.* pulchrī)	pulchrē *beautifully*
third declension	
fortis *brave* (*gen.* fortis)	fortiter *bravely*
fēlīx *lucky* (*gen.* fēlīcis)	fēlīciter *luckily*
prūdēns *shrewd* (*gen.* prūdentis)	prūdenter *shrewdly*

A few third-declension adjectives, such as *facilis* 'easy', form adverbs ending in -*e*, e.g. *facile* 'easily'.

4 Comparison

1 *comparison of adjectives*

positive (i.e. the 'normal' form of the adjective)	comparative	superlative
lātus	lātior	lātissimus
wide	*wider*	*widest, very wide*
pulcher	pulchrior	pulcherrimus
beautiful	*more beautiful*	*most beautiful, very beautiful*
fortis	fortior	fortissimus
brave	*braver*	*bravest, very brave*
fēlīx	fēlīcior	fēlīcissimus
lucky	*luckier*	*luckiest, very lucky*
prūdēns	prūdentior	prūdentissimus
shrewd	*shrewder*	*shrewdest, very shrewd*
facilis	facilior	facillimus*
easy	*easier*	*easiest, very easy*
irregular forms:		
bonus	melior	optimus
good	*better*	*best, very good*
malus	peior	pessimus
bad	*worse*	*worst, very bad*
magnus	maior	maximus
big	*bigger*	*biggest, very big*
parvus	minor	minimus
small	*smaller*	*smallest, very small*
multus	plūs	plūrimus
much	*more*	*most, very much*
multī	plūrēs	plūrimī
many	*more*	*most, very many*

Comparative adjectives such as *lātior* change their endings in the following way:

	SINGULAR		PLURAL	
	masc. and fem.	*neuter*	*masc. and fem.*	*neuter*
nominative and vocative	lātior	lātius	lātiōrēs	lātiōra
accusative	lātiōrem	lātius	lātiōrēs	lātiōra
genitive	lātiōris		lātiōrum	
dative	lātiōrī		lātiōribus	
ablative	lātiōre		lātiōribus	

Superlative adjectives such as *lātissimus* change their endings in the same way as *bonus* (shown in **2.1**).

> *plūs*, the comparative form of *multus* listed above, is a neuter singular noun meaning 'more, a greater quantity' and is often used with the genitive, e.g. *plūs cibī* 'more (of) food'.

** The adjectives *difficilis, similis, dissimilis, gracilis* and *humilis* form their superlative in the same way as *facilis*, e.g. *difficillimus, simillimus*, etc.*

2 *comparison of adverbs*

positive	*comparative*	*superlative*
lātē	lātius	lātissimē
widely	*more widely*	*most widely, very widely*
pulchrē	pulchrius	pulcherrimē
beautifully	*more beautifully*	*most beautifully, very beautifully*
fortiter	fortius	fortissimē
bravely	*more bravely*	*most bravely, very bravely*
fēlīciter	fēlīcius	fēlīcissimē
luckily	*more luckily*	*most luckily, very luckily*
prūdenter	prūdentius	prūdentissimē
shrewdly	*more shrewdly*	*most shrewdly, very shrewdly*
facile	facilius	facillimē
easily	*more easily*	*most easily, very easily*

irregular forms:

bene	melius	optimē
well	*better*	*best, very well*
male	peius	pessimē
badly	*worse*	*worst, very badly*
magnopere	magis	maximē
greatly	*more*	*most, very greatly*
paulum	minus	minimē
little	*less*	*least, very little*
multum	plūs	plūrimum
much	*more*	*most, very much*

3 Comparative forms are sometimes used with the meaning 'too . . .' or 'rather . . .':

in mediā palaestrā stābat āthlēta **altior**.
In the middle of the exercise area stood a *rather tall* athlete (i.e. an athlete *taller* than average).

mercātor iter **lentius** faciēbat.
The merchant was travelling *too slowly* (i.e. *more slowly* than he should have done).

4 Superlative forms are sometimes used with 'quam', meaning 'as . . . as possible':

quam celerrimē   as quickly as possible
quam maximus   as large as possible

5 Pronouns*

1 **ego** and **tū** 'I', 'you', 'we', etc.:

	SINGULAR		PLURAL	
nominative	ego	tū	nōs	vōs
accusative	mē	tē	nōs	vōs
genitive	meī	tuī	nostrum/nostrī	vestrum/vestrī
dative	mihi	tibi	nōbīs	vōbīs
ablative	mē	tē	nōbīs	vōbīs

sē 'himself', 'herself', 'itself', 'themselves', etc.:

	SINGULAR	PLURAL
	masc., fem. and neuter	*masc., fem. and neuter*
nominative	–	–
accusative	sē	sē
genitive	suī	suī
dative	sibi	sibi
ablative	sē	sē

mīlitēs sē īnstrūxērunt.	The soldiers drew themselves up.
senex cēnam sibi coxit.	The old man cooked a dinner for himself.
	or, The old man cooked himself a dinner.

(Compare these examples with the way *ipse* (paragraph 4) is used.)

Further examples:

1 fūr sub mēnsā sē cēlāvit.
2 captīvī sē interfēcērunt.
3 puella sibi equum ēmit.

For examples of *sē* used in indirect statements, see **25**.4d.

When *cum* 'with' is used with one of the above pronouns, it is written after the pronoun, in one word. For example:

mēcum	with me
vōbīscum	with you (plural)
sēcum	with him, with himself
	with them, with themselves

---

* including some pronominal adjectives (i.e. adjectives related to pronouns).

The possessive adjectives related to these pronouns are:

meus*   my
tuus   your (referring to one person)
noster our
vester your (referring to more than one person)
suus   his (own), her (own), its (own), their (own)

vīlla **mea** ardēbat.	My house was on fire.
amīcōs **vestrōs** vīdistis?	Have you (pl.) seen your friends?
patrem **suum** necāvit.	He killed his (own) father.
cibum līberīs **suīs** dedērunt.	They gave food to their (own) children.

(Compare the last two examples with the two examples at the end of paragraph 5.)

2   **hic** 'this', 'these', etc.; also used with the meaning 'he', 'she', 'it', 'they', etc.:

	SINGULAR			PLURAL		
	masculine	*feminine*	*neuter*	*masculine*	*feminine*	*neuter*
nominative	hic	haec	hoc	hī	hae	haec
accusative	hunc	hanc	hoc	hōs	hās	haec
genitive		huius		hōrum	hārum	hōrum
dative		huic			hīs	
ablative	hōc	hāc	hōc		hīs	

3   **ille** 'that', 'those', etc.; also used with the meaning 'he', 'she', 'it', 'they', etc.:

	SINGULAR			PLURAL		
	masculine	*feminine*	*neuter*	*masculine*	*feminine*	*neuter*
nominative	ille	illa	illud	illī	illae	illa
accusative	illum	illam	illud	illōs	illās	illa
genitive		illīus		illōrum	illārum	illōrum
dative		illī			illīs	
ablative	illō	illā	illō		illīs	

iste 'that', 'that . . . of yours', etc., sometimes used in an uncomplimentary way, changes its endings in the same way as *ille*:

istud aedificium   that building of yours
iste canis   that damned dog

* vocative masculine singular *mī*.

4   **ipse** 'myself', 'yourself', 'himself', 'itself', 'themselves', etc.:

	SINGULAR			PLURAL		
	masculine	*feminine*	*neuter*	*masculine*	*feminine*	*neuter*
nominative	ipse	ipsa	ipsum	ipsī	ipsae	ipsa
accusative	ipsum	ipsam	ipsum	ipsōs	ipsās	ipsa
genitive		ipsīus		ipsōrum	ipsārum	ipsōrum
dative		ipsī			ipsīs	
ablative	ipsō	ipsā	ipsō		ipsīs	

rēx **ipse** lacrimābat.   The king himself was weeping.
fēmina mē **ipsum** accūsāvit.   The woman accused me myself.
cōnsulēs **ipsī** aderant.   The consuls themselves were there.

▌ (Compare these examples with the way *sē* (paragraph 1) is used.)

Further examples:

1 ego ipse centuriōnem servāvī.
2 vōs ipsī in tabernā bibēbātis.
3 subitō gladiātōrēs ipsōs vīdimus.
4 dea ipsa mihi appāruit.
5 haec est statua ipsīus Caesaris.

5   **is** 'he', 'she', 'it', etc.; also used with the meaning 'that', 'those', etc.:

	SINGULAR			PLURAL		
	masculine	*feminine*	*neuter*	*masculine*	*feminine*	*neuter*
nominative	is	ea	id	eī/iī	eae	ea
accusative	eum	eam	id	eōs	eās	ea
genitive		eius		eōrum	eārum	eōrum
dative		eī			eīs/iīs	
ablative	eō	eā	eō		eīs/iīs	

▌ For examples in which forms of *is* are used with the relative pronoun *quī*, see **23**.1.

The genitive singular and plural forms of *is* can be used to mean 'his', 'her', 'its' and 'their':

patrem **eius** necāvit.
He killed his (i.e. someone else's) father.

cibum līberīs **eōrum** dedērunt.
They gave food to their (i.e. other people's) children.

▌ (Compare these examples with the last two examples in paragraph 1.)

6 **īdem** 'the same':

	SINGULAR			PLURAL		
	masculine	*feminine*	*neuter*	*masculine*	*feminine*	*neuter*
nominative	īdem	eadem	idem	eīdem/īdem	eaedem	eadem
accusative	eundem	eandem	idem	eōsdem	eāsdem	eadem
genitive		eiusdem		eōrundem	eārundem	eōrundem
dative		eīdem			eīsdem/īsdem	
ablative	eōdem	eādem	eōdem		eīsdem/īsdem	

> **eōsdem** puerōs postrīdiē audīvērunt.
> They heard the same boys on the next day.

> haec est **eiusdem** fēminae domus.
> This is the house of the same woman.

Further examples:

1 eandem puellam iterum vīdimus.
2 nūntius eōdem diē revēnit.
3 eīdem servī in agrīs labōrābant.

7 the relative pronoun **quī** 'who', 'which', etc.:

	SINGULAR			PLURAL		
	masculine	*feminine*	*neuter*	*masculine*	*feminine*	*neuter*
nominative	quī	quae	quod	quī	quae	quae
accusative	quem	quam	quod	quōs	quās	quae
genitive		cuius		quōrum	quārum	quōrum
dative		cui			quibus/quīs	
ablative	quō	quā	quō		quibus/quīs	

> For examples of agreement between the relative pronoun and a noun or
> pronoun, see **17**.4.
> For examples of clauses introduced by forms of *quī*, see **23**.1.

Forms of *quī* can also be used at the start of sentences, with the
meaning 'he', 'this', etc. (this is known as the *connecting* use of the
relative pronoun):

> tertiā hōrā dux advēnit. **quem** cum cōnspexissent, mīlitēs magnum
> clāmōrem sustulērunt.
> At the third hour the leader arrived. When they caught sight of him,
> the soldiers raised a great shout.

Continued

deinde nūntiī locūtī sunt. **quōrum** verbīs obstupefactus, rēx diū
tacēbat.
Then the messengers spoke. Stunned by their words, the king was
silent for a long time.

pontifex ipse templum dēdicāvit. **quō** factō, omnēs plausērunt.
The chief priest himself dedicated the temple. When this had been
done, everybody applauded.

Further examples:

1 rēx mihi signum dedit. quod simulac vīdī, victimam ad āram dūxī.
2 iūdex 'hic vir' inquit 'est innocēns'. quibus verbīs audītīs,
spectātōrēs īrātissimī erant.
3 dominus ancillam ad forum mīsit. quae, cum cibum comparāvisset,
ad vīllam celeriter revēnit.

> The syllable *quī*, in *aliquī* 'some', *quīcumque* 'whoever, whichever', etc.
> and *quī . . . ?* 'which . . . ?', changes its endings in the same way as the
> relative pronoun:
>
> **quī** puer fēcit?   Which boy did this?
> **aliquod** crīmen   some accusation
> **quaecumque** prōvincia   whatever province

8 **quīdam** 'one', 'a certain':

	SINGULAR			PLURAL		
	masculine	*feminine*	*neuter*	*masculine*	*feminine*	*neuter*
nominative	quīdam	quaedam	quoddam	quīdam	quaedam	quaedam
accusative	quendam	quandam	quoddam	quōsdam	quāsdam	quaedam
genitive		cuiusdam		quōrundam	quārundam	quōrundam
dative		cuidam			quibusdam	
ablative	quōdam	quādam	quōdam		quibusdam	

mīlitem **quendam** dormientem animadvertit.
He noticed one soldier sleeping.

in vīllā **cuiusdam** amīcī manēbāmus.
We were staying in the villa of a certain friend.

Further examples:

1 fēminae quaedam extrā iānuam stābant.
2 senātor quīdam subitō surrēxit.
3 quōsdam hominēs in forō cōnspexī.

9 **quis? quid?** 'who? what?':

	SINGULAR			PLURAL		
	masculine	*feminine*	*neuter*	*masculine*	*feminine*	*neuter*
nominative	quis	quis	quid	quī	quae	quae
accusative	quem	quam	quid	quōs	quās	quae
genitive		cuius		quōrum	quārum	quōrum
dative		cui			quibus	
ablative	quō	quā	quō		quibus	

The forms of *quis* can also be used with *sī*, *nisi*, *nē* and *num* to mean 'anyone', 'anything':

> sī **quis** restiterit, comprehende eum!
> If anybody resists, arrest him!

> centuriō mē rogāvit num **quid** vīdissem.
> The centurion asked me whether I had seen anything.

> The syllable *quis*, in *quisquam* 'any' (used after negative words), *quisque* 'each', *quisquis* 'whoever' and *aliquis*, *aliquid* 'someone, something', changes its endings in the same way as *quis?*:
>
> | | |
> |---|---|
> | **quidquid** accidit, semper rīdet. | Whatever happens, he always smiles. |
> | **aliquis** clāmābat. | Someone was shouting. |
> | neque **quemquam** vīdī. | Nor did I see anybody. |
> | | *or*, in more natural English: |
> | | And I didn't see anybody. |
> | prō sē **quisque** pugnābat. | Each one was fighting for himself. |
>
> *quisque* is also used with superlative adjectives in the following way:
>
> | | |
> |---|---|
> | optimus **quisque** | each very good man, i.e. all the best men |
> | celerrimus **quisque** | each very fast person, i.e. all the fastest people |

10 The following words change most of their endings in the same way as 1st and 2nd declension adjectives like *bonus*, *pulcher* and *miser* (shown in **2.1**), but have a genitive singular ending in *-īus* and a dative singular ending in *-ī*:

ūnus	one (shown in full in **6.1**)		
nūllus	no, none	alter	the other (of two)
sōlus	alone	alius*	another
tōtus	whole	uter?	which (of two)?
ūllus	any	neuter	neither

uterque 'each', 'both' has genitive singular *utrīusque* and dative singular *utrīque*.

---

*nominative, vocative and accusative neuter singular *aliud*

11 **nēmō** 'no one':

nominative	nēmō
accusative	nēminem
genitive	nūllīus
dative	nēminī
ablative	nūllō

12 *Exercise* With the help of paragraphs 1–11, work out the Latin for the italicised words:

1 *That* old man is the consul.
2 *What* has happened?
3 I found *no one* there.
4 We were detained in the city by *certain* business (*negōtium* is neuter).
5 The queen stabbed *herself*.
6 The soldiers seized the queen *herself*.
7 I again gave my message, to *the same* slave as before.
8 He ran after the men, but couldn't catch *them*.
9 Where is *this* horse's owner?
10 I will tell *you* the reason, my friends.
11 Three slave-girls ran up, with *whose* help the fire was extinguished.
12 He became king of the *whole* island.

6 Numerals

1

I	ūnus	1	XX	vīgintī	20
II	duo	2	XXX	trīgintā	30
III	trēs	3	XL	quadrāgintā	40
IV	quattuor	4	L	quīnquāgintā	50
V	quīnque	5	LX	sexāgintā	60
VI	sex	6	LXX	septuāgintā	70
VII	septem	7	LXXX	octōgintā	80
VIII	octō	8	XC	nōnāgintā	90
IX	novem	9	C	centum	100
X	decem	10	CC	ducentī	200
XI	ūndecim	11	CCC	trecentī	300
XII	duodecim	12	CCCC	quadringentī	400
XIII	trēdecim	13	D	quīngentī	500
XIV	quattuordecim	14	DC	sescentī	600
XV	quīndecim	15	DCC	septingentī	700
XVI	sēdecim	16	DCCC	octingentī	800
XVII	septendecim	17	DCCCC	nōngentī	900
XVIII	duodēvīgintī	18	M	mīlle	1000
XIX	ūndēvīgintī	19	MM	duo mīlia	2000

Compound numbers below 100 (e.g. 46, 63, 95) can be formed *either* with the smaller number first, followed by *et* and the larger number, *or* with the larger number first, followed by the smaller number without *et*:

quīnque et trīgintā *or* trīgintā quīnque   35
septem et octōgintā *or* octōgintā septem   87*

28, 29, 38, 39, 48, 49, etc. are usually formed as follows:

duodētrīgintā   28   ūndētrīgintā   29
duodēquadrāgintā   38   ūndēquadrāgintā   39   etc.†

In compound numbers above 100, the larger number is placed in front of the smaller number, with or without *et*:

ducentī et sex *or* ducentī sex   206

ūnus, *duo* and *trēs* change their endings in the following way:

	masculine	feminine	neuter	masculine	feminine	neuter
nominative	ūnus	ūna	ūnum	duo	duae	duo
accusative	ūnum	ūnam	ūnum	duōs/duo	duās	duo
genitive		ūnīus		duōrum	duārum	duōrum
dative		ūnī		duōbus	duābus	duōbus
ablative	ūnō	ūnā ·	ūnō	duōbus	duābus	duōbus

ambō 'both' changes its endings in the same way as *duo*.   *Continued*

* ūnus is generally placed first:
ūnus et quīnquāgintā   51

†But octō et nōnāgintā ⎫
   or nōnāgintā octō ⎭   98   ūndēcentum   99

	masc. and fem.	neuter
nominative	trēs	tria
accusative	trēs	tria
genitive	trium	
dative	tribus	
ablative	tribus	

The numbers from *quattuor* to *centum* do not change their endings. *ducentī*, *trecentī*, etc. change their endings in the same way as the plural of *bonus* (shown in **2**.1).

mīlle does not change its endings:

> **mīlle** servī a thousand slaves
> cum **mīlle** servīs with a thousand slaves

mīlia changes its endings in the same way as the plural of *mare* (shown in **1**.3), and is used with a noun in the genitive case:

> sex **mīlia** servōrum six thousand(s) (of) slaves
> cum sex **mīlibus** servōrum with six thousand(s) (of) slaves

2
prīmus	first	sextus	sixth
secundus	second	septimus	seventh
tertius	third	octāvus	eighth
quārtus	fourth	nōnus	ninth
quīntus	fifth	decimus	tenth

prīmus, *secundus*, etc. change their endings in the same way as *bonus*.

3
singulī	one each	sēnī	six each
bīnī	two each	septēnī	seven each
ternī	three each	octōnī	eight each
quaternī	four each	novēnī	nine each
quīnī	five each	dēnī	ten each

These numbers change their endings in the same way as the plural of *bonus*.

4
semel	once	sexiēs	six times
bis	twice	septiēs	seven times
ter	three times	octiēs	eight times
quater	four times	noviēs	nine times
quīnquiēs	five times	deciēs	ten times

7 Verbs

7a Summary of verb forms

s. = singular   pl. = plural
1, 2, 3 = 1st, 2nd and 3rd person (meaning 'I . . .', 'you . . .' and 'he, she, it . . .'
in the singular and 'we . . .', 'you . . .' and 'they . . .' in the plural)

Indicative active

PRESENT s. { 1 2 3 } pl. { 1 2 3 }

FUTURE s. { 1 2 3 } pl. { 1 2 3 }

IMPERFECT s. { 1 2 3 } pl. { 1 2 3 }

PERFECT s. { 1 2 3 } pl. { 1 2 3 }

FUTURE PERFECT s. { 1 2 3 } pl. { 1 2 3 }

PLUPERFECT s. { 1 2 3 } pl. { 1 2 3 }

Indicative passive

PRESENT s. { 1 2 3 } pl. { 1 2 3 }

FUTURE s. { 1 2 3 } pl. { 1 2 3 }

IMPERFECT s. { 1 2 3 } pl. { 1 2 3 }

PERFECT s. { 1 2 3 } pl. { 1 2 3 }

FUTURE PERFECT s. { 1 2 3 } pl. { 1 2 3 }

PLUPERFECT s. { 1 2 3 } pl. { 1 2 3 }

Imperative active	*Imperative passive*
singular and plural	singular and plural

Infinitives (active)	*Infinitives (passive)*
present	present
perfect	perfect
future	future

Participles (active)	*Participle (passive)*
present	perfect
future	

Miscellaneous (active)	*Miscellaneous (passive)*
gerund	gerundive
supine	

Subjunctive active

PRESENT s. { 1 2 3 } pl. { 1 2 3 }

IMPERFECT s. { 1 2 3 } pl. { 1 2 3 }

PERFECT s. { 1 2 3 } pl. { 1 2 3 }

PLUPERFECT s. { 1 2 3 } pl. { 1 2 3 }

Subjunctive passive

PRESENT s. { 1 2 3 } pl. { 1 2 3 }

IMPERFECT s. { 1 2 3 } pl. { 1 2 3 }

PERFECT s. { 1 2 3 } pl. { 1 2 3 }

PLUPERFECT s. { 1 2 3 } pl. { 1 2 3 }

7b Indicative active forms of:

portō 'I carry'   **audiō** 'I hear'   **trahō** 'I drag'
doceō 'I teach'   **capiō** 'I take, I capture'

1*

first conjugation	second conjugation	third conjugation	fourth conjugation	mixed conjugation
PRESENT (*'I carry', 'I am carrying', etc.*)				
portō	doceō	trahō	audiō	*capiō*
portās	docēs	trahis	audīs	capis
portat	docet	trahit	audit	capit
portāmus	docēmus	trahimus	audīmus	capimus
portātis	docētis	trahitis	audītis	capitis
portant	docent	trahunt	audiunt	*capiunt*
FUTURE (*'I shall carry', etc.*)				
portābō	docēbō	traham	audiam	*capiam*
portābis	docēbis	trahēs	audiēs	*capiēs*
portābit	docēbit	trahet	audiet	*capiet*
portābimus	docēbimus	trahēmus	audiēmus	*capiēmus*
portābitis	docēbitis	trahētis	audiētis	*capiētis*
portābunt	docēbunt	trahent	audient	*capient*
IMPERFECT (*'I was carrying', 'I used to carry', 'I began to carry', etc.*)				
portābam	docēbam	trahēbam	audiēbam	*capiēbam*
portābās	docēbās	trahēbās	audiēbās	*capiēbās*
portābat	docēbat	trahēbat	audiēbat	*capiēbat*
portābāmus	docēbāmus	trahēbāmus	audiēbāmus	*capiēbāmus*
portābātis	docēbātis	trahēbātis	audiēbātis	*capiēbātis*
portābant	docēbant	trahēbant	audiēbant	*capiēbant*

2 *capiō* belongs to a group of verbs which form some of their endings like third-conjugation verbs such as *trahō* but form other endings (italicised) like fourth-conjugation verbs such as *audiō*. (Other common verbs in this group are *faciō*, *iaciō* and *rapiō*; for further examples, see **34**.5.)

3 The *historic* use of the present tense (*'historic present'* for short) is often employed by Roman writers as a lively or vivid way of describing events that happened in the past:

> fūr per fenestram intrāvit. circumspexit; sed omnia tacita erant. subitō sonitum **audit**; ē tablīnō canis sē **praecipitat**. fūr effugere **cōnātur**; **lātrat** canis; **irrumpunt** servī et fūrem **comprehendunt**.

> A thief entered through the window. He looked round; but all was silent. Suddenly he *hears* a noise; a dog *hurtles* out of the study. The thief *tries* to escape; the dog *barks*; the slaves *rush in* and *seize* the thief.

A historic present in Latin can be translated *either* by an English present tense (as in the example above), *or* by a past tense.

---

*The endings of each tense are listed in the standard order, i.e. 1st, 2nd and 3rd person singular endings, followed by 1st, 2nd and 3rd person plural.

4 The present tense is also used to indicate an action which has begun earlier and is still going on; it is usually translated by an English perfect tense:

trēs hōrās eum **exspectō**! *I have been waiting* for him for three hours!

5 PERFECT (*'I have carried', 'I carried', etc.*)

portāvī	docuī	trāxī	audīvī	cēpī
portāvistī	docuistī	trāxistī	audīvistī	cēpistī
portāvit	docuit	trāxit	audīvit	cēpit
portāvimus	docuimus	trāximus	audīvimus	cēpimus
portāvistis	docuistis	trāxistis	audīvistis	cēpistis
portāvērunt	docuērunt	trāxērunt	audīvērunt	cēpērunt

FUTURE PERFECT (*'I shall have carried', etc.*)

portāverō	docuerō	trāxerō	audīverō	cēperō
portāveris	docueris	trāxeris	audīveris	cēperis
portāverit	docuerit	trāxerit	audīverit	cēperit
portāverimus	docuerimus	trāxerimus	audīverimus	cēperimus
portāveritis	docueritis	trāxeritis	audīveritis	cēperitis
portāverint	docuerint	trāxerint	audīverint	cēperint

PLUPERFECT (*'I had carried', etc.*)

portāveram	docueram	trāxeram	audīveram	cēperam
portāverās	docuerās	trāxerās	audīverās	cēperās
portāverat	docuerat	trāxerat	audīverat	cēperat
portāverāmus	docuerāmus	trāxerāmus	audīverāmus	cēperāmus
portāverātis	docuerātis	trāxerātis	audīverātis	cēperātis
portāverant	docuerant	trāxerant	audīverant	cēperant

6 The 3rd person plural form of the perfect tense sometimes ends in *-ēre* instead of *-ērunt*:

portāvēre = portāvērunt = they (have) carried
trāxēre = trāxērunt = they (have) dragged

Further examples: audīvēre; salūtāvēre; discessēre; monuēre.
This way of forming the 3rd person plural of the perfect is especially common in verse.

7 1st-conjugation verbs whose perfect tense is normally formed with the letter *-v-* sometimes shorten the endings of their perfect, future perfect and pluperfect tenses. For example:

portāstī = portāvistī = you (have) carried
laudārat = laudāverat = he had praised

4th-conjugation verbs sometimes omit *-v-* in their perfect, future perfect and pluperfect tenses. For example:

audiī = audīvī = I (have) heard

8 The future perfect tense is usually translated by an English present or perfect tense, to suit the sense of the sentence in which it occurs:

sī mē **rogāverit**, respondēbō. If he *asks* me, I'll reply.
cum eum **vīderis**, redī. When you *have seen* him, come back.

7c Indicative passive

1

PRESENT *('I am carried', etc.)*

portor	doceor	trahor	audior	*capior*
portāris	docēris	traheris*	audīris	*caperis*
portātur	docētur	trahitur	audītur	*capitur*
portāmur	docēmur	trahimur	audīmur	*capimur*
portāminī	docēminī	trahiminī	audīminī	*capiminī*
portantur	docentur	trahuntur	audiuntur	*capiuntur*

FUTURE *('I shall be carried', etc.)*

portābor	docēbor	trahar	audiar	*capiar*
portāberis	docēberis	trahēris*	audiēris	*capiēris*
portābitur	docēbitur	trahētur	audiētur	*capiētur*
portābimur	docēbimur	trahēmur	audiēmur	*capiēmur*
portābiminī	docēbiminī	trahēminī	audiēminī	*capiēminī*
portābuntur	docēbuntur	trahentur	audientur	*capientur*

IMPERFECT *('I was being carried', 'I used to be carried', etc.)*

portābar	docēbar	trahēbar	audiēbar	*capiēbar*
portābāris	docēbāris	trahēbāris	audiēbāris	*capiēbāris*
portābātur	docēbātur	trahēbātur	audiēbātur	*capiēbātur*
portābāmur	docēbāmur	trahēbāmur	audiēbāmur	*capiēbāmur*
portābāminī	docēbāminī	trahēbāminī	audiēbāminī	*capiēbāminī*
portābantur	docēbantur	trahēbantur	audiēbantur	*capiēbantur*

> The 2nd person singular form of the future and imperfect tenses of the passive sometimes ends in -re instead of -ris:
>
> docēbere = docēberis = you will be taught
> audiēre = audiēris = you will be heard
> trahēbāre = trahēbāris = you were being dragged

---

*Compare the pronunciation of *traheris* 'you are being dragged' and *trahēris* 'you will be dragged'.

2

PERFECT *('I have been carried', 'I was carried', etc.)*

portātus sum	doctus sum	tractus sum	audītus sum	captus sum
portātus es	doctus es	tractus es	audītus es	captus es
portātus est	doctus est	tractus est	audītus est	captus est
portātī sumus	doctī sumus	tractī sumus	audītī sumus	captī sumus
portātī estis	doctī estis	tractī estis	audītī estis	captī estis
portātī sunt	doctī sunt	tractī sunt	audītī sunt	captī sunt

FUTURE PERFECT *('I shall have been carried', etc., but usually translated by an English present or perfect tense)*

portātus erō	doctus erō	tractus erō	audītus erō	captus erō
portātus eris	doctus eris	tractus eris	audītus eris	captus eris
portātus erit	doctus erit	tractus erit	audītus erit	captus erit
portātī erimus	doctī erimus	tractī erimus	audītī erimus	captī erimus
portātī eritis	doctī eritis	tractī eritis	audītī eritis	captī eritis
portātī erunt	doctī erunt	tractī erunt	audītī erunt	captī erunt

PLUPERFECT *('I had been carried', etc.)*

portātus eram	doctus eram	tractus eram	audītus eram	captus eram
portātus erās	doctus erās	tractus erās	audītus erās	captus erās
portātus erat	doctus erat	tractus erat	audītus erat	captus erat
portātī erāmus	doctī erāmus	tractī erāmus	audītī erāmus	captī erāmus
portātī erātis	doctī erātis	tractī erātis	audītī erātis	captī erātis
portātī erant	doctī erant	tractī erant	audītī erant	captī erant

3   The tenses in paragraph 2 are formed with perfect passive participles, which change their endings to indicate number and gender. For example:

audītus est.	He was heard.
audīta est.	She was heard.
audītum est.	It was heard.
audītī sunt.	They (masc.) were heard.
audītae sunt.	They (fem.) were heard.
audīta sunt.	They (neut.) were heard.

4   *Exercise*   With the help (if necessary) of **7b** and paragraphs 1 and 2 translate:

1 audīveram.	5 trāxit.	9 audiēbāminī.
2 portābāmus.	6 capiētis.	10 captī erāmus.
3 docēs.	7 trahor.	
4 docēbunt.	8 portātī sunt.	

In **7b** and paragraphs 1 and 2, find the Latin for:

11 He captures.	16 He was hearing.
12 They will drag.	17 You (pl.) will be taught.
13 We have been carried.	18 We drag.
14 You (s.) were being taught.	19 I had been carried.
15 I shall have been heard.	20 You (pl.) have captured.

7d Subjunctive active

1

PRESENT				
portem	doceam	traham	audiam	*capiam*
portēs	doceās	trahās	audiās	*capiās*
portet	doceat	trahat	audiat	*capiat*
portēmus	doceāmus	trahāmus	audiāmus	*capiāmus*
portētis	doceātis	trahātis	audiātis	*capiātis*
portent	doceant	trahant	audiant	*capiant*

IMPERFECT				
portārem	docērem	traherem	audīrem	caperem
portārēs	docērēs	traherēs	audīrēs	caperēs
portāret	docēret	traheret	audīret	caperet
portārēmus	docērēmus	traherēmus	audīrēmus	caperēmus
portārētis	docērētis	traherētis	audīrētis	caperētis
portārent	docērent	traherent	audīrent	caperent

PERFECT				
portāverim	docuerim	trāxerim	audīverim	cēperim
portāverīs	docuerīs	trāxerīs	audīverīs	cēperīs
portāverit	docuerit	trāxerit	audīverit	cēperit
portāverīmus	docuerīmus	trāxerīmus	audīverīmus	cēperīmus
portāverītis	docuerītis	trāxerītis	audīverītis	cēperītis
portāverint	docuerint	trāxerint	audīverint	cēperint

PLUPERFECT				
portāvissem	docuissem	trāxissem	audīvissem	cēpissem
portāvissēs	docuissēs	trāxissēs	audīvissēs	cēpissēs
portāvisset	docuisset	trāxisset	audīvisset	cēpisset
portāvissēmus	docuissēmus	trāxissēmus	audīvissēmus	cēpissēmus
portāvissētis	docuissētis	trāxissētis	audīvissētis	cēpissētis
portāvissent	docuissent	trāxissent	audīvissent	cēpissent

2 ▌ For examples of ways in which the subjunctive is used, see **33**.1–2.

3 There are many different ways of translating the subjunctive, especially in the present and imperfect tenses; the correct translation always depends on the way the subjunctive is being used in the sentence. The perfect and pluperfect subjunctive tenses, e.g. *portāverim* and *audīvissem*, are usually (but not always) translated in the same way as the perfect and pluperfect indicative, e.g. 'I have carried', 'I had heard', etc.

4 The subjunctive has no future or future perfect tenses. Instead, the future participle is used with the present or imperfect subjunctive of *sum* ('I am'):

> nesciunt quandō amīcus tuus **adventūrus sit**.
> They do not know when your friend is going to arrive.
> *or*, They do not know when your friend will arrive.

in animō volvēbam quid **vīsūrus essem**.
I was wondering what I was going to see.
or, I was wondering what I would see.

5   Some verbs (see **7b**.7) can shorten the forms of their perfect and
pluperfect subjunctive tenses. For example:

portāssem = portāvissem   audierit = audīverit

7e Subjunctive passive

PRESENT				
porter	docear	trahar	audiar	*capiar*
portēris	doceāris	trahāris	audiāris	*capiāris*
portētur	doceātur	trahātur	audiātur	*capiātur*
portēmur	doceāmur	trahāmur	audiāmur	*capiāmur*
portēminī	doceāminī	trahāminī	audiāminī	*capiāminī*
portentur	doceantur	trahantur	audiantur	*capiantur*
IMPERFECT				
portārer	docērer	traherer	audīrer	caperer
portārēris	docērēris	traherēris	audīrēris	caperēris
portārētur	docērētur	traherētur	audīrētur	caperētur
portārēmur	docērēmur	traherēmur	audīrēmur	caperēmur
portārēminī	docērēminī	traherēminī	audīrēminī	caperēminī
portārentur	docērentur	traherentur	audīrentur	caperentur
PERFECT				
portātus sim	doctus sim	tractus sim	audītus sim	captus sim
portātus sīs	doctus sīs	tractus sīs	audītus sīs	captus sīs
portātus sit	doctus sit	tractus sit	audītus sit	captus sit
portātī sīmus	doctī sīmus	tractī sīmus	audītī sīmus	captī sīmus
portātī sītis	doctī sītis	tractī sītis	audītī sītis	captī sītis
portātī sint	doctī sint	tractī sint	audītī sint	captī sint
PLUPERFECT				
portātus essem	doctus essem	tractus essem	audītus essem	captus essem
portātus essēs	doctus essēs	tractus essēs	audītus essēs	captus essēs
portātus esset	doctus esset	tractus esset	audītus esset	captus esset
portātī essēmus	doctī essēmus	tractī essēmus	audītī essēmus	captī essēmus
portātī essētis	doctī essētis	tractī essētis	audītī essētis	captī essētis
portātī essent	doctī essent	tractī essent	audītī essent	captī essent

The 2nd person singular form of the present and imperfect tenses of the
subjunctive passive sometimes ends in -*re* instead of -*ris*:

PRESENT: portēre = portēris, doceāre = doceāris, etc.
IMPERFECT: portārēre = portārēris, docērēre = docērēris, etc.

7f Other forms of the verb

1 IMPERATIVE ACTIVE *('carry!', etc.)*

*singular**	portā	docē	trahe	audī	cape
plural	portāte	docēte	trahite	audīte	capite

2 IMPERATIVE PASSIVE *('be carried!', etc.)*

singular	portāre	docēre	trahere	audīre	capere
plural	portāminī	docēminī	trahiminī	audīminī	capiminī

3 PRESENT PARTICIPLE *('carrying', etc.)*

portāns   docēns   trahēns   audiēns   *capiēns*

Present participles change their endings in the same way as *ingēns* (shown in **2.2**), except for their ablative singular, which sometimes ends in *-e*, sometimes in *-ī*. It ends in *-ī* when the participle is being used as an adjective, e.g. *ā puerō dormientī* 'by the sleeping boy'; but it ends in *-e* when it is used in an ablative absolute phrase, e.g. *puerō dormiente* 'while the boy sleeps'.

4 PERFECT PASSIVE PARTICIPLE *('having been carried', etc.)*

portātus   doctus   tractus   audītus   captus

▌ For perfect *active* participles, see Deponent verbs, **8c.3**.

5 FUTURE PARTICIPLE *('about to carry', etc.)*

portātūrus doctūrus   tractūrus   audītūrus   captūrus

Perfect passive and future participles change their endings in the same way as *bonus* (shown in **2.1**).

▌ For examples of ways in which participles are used, see **20.1–10**.

6 PRESENT ACTIVE INFINITIVE *('to carry', etc.)*

portāre   docēre   trahere   audīre   capere

7 PRESENT PASSIVE INFINITIVE *('to be carried', etc.)*

portārī   docērī   trahī   audīrī   capī

8 PERFECT ACTIVE INFINITIVE *('to have carried', etc.)*

{ portāvisse docuisse   trāxisse   { audīvisse   cēpisse
{ *sometimes* portāsse   { *sometimes* audīsse

9 PERFECT PASSIVE INFINITIVE *('to have been carried', etc.)*

portātus esse doctus esse   tractus esse   audītus esse   captus esse

portātus, doctus, tractus, etc. change their endings to agree with the nouns which they refer to.

---

* The verbs *dīcō, dūcō* and *faciō* have a short form of the imperative singular: *dīc!* 'say! tell!', *dūc!* 'lead! take!' and *fac!* 'do! make!'

10 FUTURE ACTIVE INFINITIVE *('to be about to carry', etc.)*
portātūrus esse   doctūrus esse   tractūrus esse   audītūrus esse   captūrus esse

portātūrus, doctūrus, etc. change their endings to agree with the nouns which they refer to.

11 FUTURE PASSIVE INFINITIVE *('to be about to be carried', etc.)*
portātum īrī   doctum īrī   tractum īrī   audītum īrī   captum īrī

The endings of *portātum, doctum*, etc. in the future passive infinitive do not change.

For examples of ways in which infinitives are used, see **21**.1–8 and **25**.4.

12 GERUND *('carrying', etc.)*

nominative	–	–	–	–	–
accusative	portandum	docendum	trahendum	audiendum	*capiendum*
genitive	portandī	docendī	trahendī	audiendī	*capiendī*
dative	portandō	docendō	trahendō	audiendō	*capiendō*
ablative	portandō	docendō	trahendō	audiendō	*capiendō*

The gerund has no nominative case and no plural.

13 GERUNDIVE *('being carried', 'needing to be carried', etc.)*
portandus   docendus   trahendus   audiendus   *capiendus*

Gerundives change their endings in the same way as *bonus* (shown in **2**.1).

14 SUPINE *(for translation, see 26.3)*

accusative	portātum	doctum	tractum	audītum	captum
ablative	portātū	doctū	tractū	audītū	captū

For examples of ways in which the gerund, gerundive and supine are used, see **26**.1–3.

8 Deponent verbs

(i.e. verbs which have passive forms and active meanings)

8a Indicative forms of

cōnor	'I try'	**mentior**	'I lie, I tell a lie'
vereor	'I fear'	**patior**	'I suffer'
loquor	'I speak'		

1

first conjugation	second conjugation	third conjugation	fourth conjugation	mixed conjugation
PRESENT *('I try', 'I am trying', etc.)*				
cōnor	vereor	loquor	mentior	*patior*
cōnāris	verēris	loqueris	mentīris	pateris
cōnātur	verētur	loquitur	mentītur	patitur
cōnāmur	verēmur	loquimur	mentīmur	patimur
cōnāminī	verēminī	loquiminī	mentīminī	patiminī
cōnantur	verentur	loquuntur	mentiuntur	*patiuntur*
FUTURE *('I shall try', etc.)*				
cōnābor	verēbor	loquar	mentiar	*patiar*
cōnāberis	verēberis	loquēris	mentiēris	*patiēris*
cōnābitur	verēbitur	loquētur	mentiētur	*patiētur*
cōnābimur	verēbimur	loquēmur	mentiēmur	*patiēmur*
cōnābiminī	verēbiminī	loquēminī	mentiēminī	*patiēminī*
cōnābuntur	verēbuntur	loquentur	mentientur	*patientur*
IMPERFECT *('I was trying', 'I used to try', etc.)*				
cōnābar	verēbar	loquēbar	mentiēbar	*patiēbar*
cōnābāris	verēbāris	loquēbāris	mentiēbāris	*patiēbāris*
cōnābātur	verēbātur	loquēbātur	mentiēbātur	*patiēbātur*
cōnābāmur	verēbāmur	loquēbāmur	mentiēbāmur	*patiēbāmur*
cōnābāminī	verēbāminī	loquēbāminī	mentiēbāminī	*patiēbāminī*
cōnābantur	verēbantur	loquēbantur	mentiēbantur	*patiēbantur*

Compare these and other forms of *cōnor, vereor, loquor, mentior* and *patior* with the PASSIVE forms of *portō, doceō, trahō, audiō* and *capiō* (shown in **7c.**1–2, **7e** and **7f**).

2 *patior* belongs to a group of deponent verbs which form some of their endings like third-conjugation verbs such as *loquor* but form other endings (italicised) like fourth-conjugation verbs such as *mentior*. Other common verbs in this group are *gradior* and its compounds (e.g. *ēgredior, ingredior* and other verbs listed in **34.**5e) and *morior*.

PERFECT *('I have tried', 'I tried', etc.)*

cōnātus sum	veritus sum	locūtus sum	mentītus sum	passus sum
cōnātus es	veritus es	locūtus es	mentītus es	passus es
cōnātus est	veritus est	locūtus est	mentītus est	passus est
cōnātī sumus	veritī sumus	locūtī sumus	mentītī sumus	passī sumus
cōnātī estis	veritī estis	locūtī estis	mentītī estis	passī estis
cōnātī sunt	veritī sunt	locūtī sunt	mentītī sunt	passī sunt

FUTURE PERFECT *('I shall have tried', etc., but often translated by an English present or perfect tense)*

cōnātus erō	veritus erō	locūtus erō	mentītus erō	passus erō
cōnātus eris	veritus eris	locūtus eris	mentītus eris	passus eris
etc.	*etc.*	*etc.*	*etc.*	*etc.*

PLUPERFECT *('I had tried', etc.)*

cōnātus eram	veritus eram	locūtus eram	mentītus eram	passus eram
cōnātus erās	veritus erās	locūtus erās	mentītus erās	passus erās
etc.	*etc.*	*etc.*	*etc.*	*etc.*

3 *Exercise* With the help (if necessary) of paragraphs 1 and 2 opposite translate:

1 cōnābantur.
2 locūtus eram.
3 patiminī.
4 veritus est.
5 mentiēmur.
6 verēbitur.

In paragraphs 1 and 2, find the Latin for:

7 We try.
8 I have suffered.
9 You (pl.) were speaking.
10 You (s.) had feared.
11 He will suffer.
12 They told lies.

8b Subjunctive

PRESENT

cōner	verear	loquar	mentiar	*patiar*
cōnēris	vereāris	loquāris	mentiāris	*patiāris*
cōnētur	vereātur	loquātur	mentiātur	*patiātur*
cōnēmur	vereāmur	loquāmur	mentiāmur	*patiāmur*
cōnēminī	vereāminī	loquāminī	mentiāminī	*patiāminī*
cōnentur	vereantur	loquantur	mentiantur	*patiantur*

IMPERFECT

cōnārer	verērer	loquerer	mentīrer	paterer
cōnārēris	verērēris	loquerēris	mentīrēris	paterēris
cōnārētur	verērētur	loquerētur	mentīrētur	paterētur
cōnārēmur	verērēmur	loquerēmur	mentīrēmur	paterēmur
cōnārēminī	verērēminī	loquerēminī	mentīrēminī	paterēminī
cōnārentur	verērentur	loquerentur	mentīrentur	paterentur

PERFECT

cōnātus sim	veritus sim	locūtus sim	mentītus sim	passus sim
cōnātus sīs	veritus sīs	locūtus sīs	mentītus sīs	passus sīs
etc.	*etc.*	*etc.*	*etc.*	*etc.*

PLUPERFECT

cōnātus essem	veritus essem	locūtus essem	mentītus essem	passus essem
cōnātus essēs	veritus essēs	locūtus essēs	mentītus essēs	passus essēs
etc.	*etc.*	*etc.*	*etc.*	*etc.*

8c Other forms

1 IMPERATIVE (*'try!'*, etc.)

singular	cōnāre	verēre	loquere	mentīre	patere
plural	cōnāminī	verēminī	loquiminī	mentīminī	patiminī

2 PRESENT PARTICIPLE (*'trying'*, etc.)

cōnāns	verēns	loquēns	mentiēns	*patiēns*

3 PERFECT ACTIVE PARTICIPLE (*'having tried'*, etc.)

cōnātus	veritus	locūtus	mentītus	passus

4 FUTURE PARTICIPLE (*'about to try'*, etc.)

cōnātūrus	veritūrus	locūtūrus	mentītūrus	passūrus

Perfect active and future participles change their endings in the same way as *bonus* (shown in **2.1**).

5 PRESENT INFINITIVE *('to try', etc.)*
  cōnārī   verērī   loquī   mentīrī   patī

6 PERFECT INFINITIVE *('to have tried', etc.)*
  cōnātus esse   veritus esse   locūtus esse   mentītus esse   passus esse

7 FUTURE INFINITIVE *('to be about to try', etc.)*
  cōnātūrus esse   veritūrus esse   locūtūrus esse   mentītūrus esse   passūrus esse

8 GERUND *('trying', etc.)*
  cōnandum verendum   loquendum   mentiendum   *patiendum*

9 GERUNDIVE *(for translation, see* **26.2***)*
  cōnandus verendus   loquendus   mentiendus   *patiendus*

10 SUPINE *(for translation, see* **26.3***)*
  cōnātum   veritum   locūtum   mentītum   passum

The gerund, gerundive and supine of deponent verbs change their endings in the same way as those of *portō*, *doceō*, etc. (shown in **7f.** 12–14).

> Deponent verbs normally have passive forms but active meanings. The only exceptions are the present and future participles, future infinitive, gerund and supine, which have active forms (e.g. *cōnāns, cōnātūrus, cōnātūrus esse, cōnandum* and *cōnātum*) and the gerundive, which has a passive meaning (e.g. *loquendus* 'being spoken, needing to be spoken').

8d Semi-deponent verbs

A few verbs, such as *audeō* 'I dare', are known as *semi-deponent verbs*, because they form their present, future and imperfect tenses in the ordinary way, but form their perfect, future perfect and pluperfect like deponent verbs, i.e. with passive forms and active meanings. For example:

audeō   I dare   audēbō   I shall dare   audēbam   I was daring
ausus sum I dared   ausus erō   I shall have dared   ausus eram I had dared
                     audēns daring   ausus   having dared

Other semi-deponent verbs are *cōnfīdō*, *gaudeō* and *soleō*:

cōnfīdō   I trust   cōnfīsus sum   I trusted
gaudeō   I rejoice, I am glad gāvīsus sum   I rejoiced, I was glad
soleō   I am accustomed   solitus sum   I was accustomed

9 Irregular verbs

1 *Indicative* forms of

sum	'I am'		**volō**	'I want'
possum	'I am able'		**ferō**	'I bring'
eō	'I go'		**fīō**	'I am made, I become'

PRESENT *('I am', etc.)*

sum	possum	eō	volō*	ferō	fīō
es	potes	īs	vīs	fers	fīs
est	potest	it	vult	fert	fit
sumus	possumus	īmus	volumus	ferimus	–
estis	potestis	ītis	vultis	fertis	–
sunt	possunt	eunt	volunt	ferunt	fīunt

FUTURE *('I shall be', etc.)*

erō	poterō	ībō	volam	feram	fīam
eris	poteris	ībis	volēs	ferēs	fīēs
erit	poterit	ībit	volet	feret	fīet
erimus	poterimus	ībimus	volēmus	ferēmus	fīēmus
eritis	poteritis	ībitis	volētis	ferētis	fīētis
erunt	poterunt	ībunt	volent	ferent	fīent

IMPERFECT *('I was', etc.)*

eram	poteram	ībam	volēbam	ferēbam	fīēbam
erās	poterās	ībās	volēbās	ferēbās	fīēbās
erat	poterat	ībat	volēbat	ferēbat	fīēbat
erāmus	poterāmus	ībāmus	volēbāmus	ferēbāmus	fīēbāmus
erātis	poterātis	ībātis	volēbātis	ferēbātis	fīēbātis
erant	poterant	ībant	volēbant	ferēbant	fīēbant

PERFECT *('I have been', etc.)*

fuī	potuī	iī[§]	voluī	tulī	†
fuistī	potuistī	iistī[§]	voluistī	tulistī	
etc.	*etc.*	*etc.*	*etc.*	*etc.*	

FUTURE PERFECT *('I shall have been', etc.)*

fuerō	potuerō	ierō[§]	voluerō	tulerō	†
fueris	potueris	ieris[§]	volueris	tuleris	
etc.	*etc.*	*etc.*	*etc.*	*etc.*	

PLUPERFECT *('I had been', etc.)*

fueram	potueram	ieram[§]	volueram	tuleram	†
fuerās	potuerās	ierās[§]	voluerās	tulerās	
etc.	*etc.*	*etc.*	*etc.*	*etc.*	

* For examples of forms of *nōlō* 'I do not want' and *mālō* 'I prefer', see **9.6**.

§ Sometimes *īvī, īvistī, īverō, īveris, īveram, īverās*, etc.

† For these tenses, passive forms of *faciō* are used, e.g. *factus sum* 'I was made, I became'.

2 *Subjunctive*

PRESENT SUBJUNCTIVE

sim	possim	eam	velim	feram	fīam
sīs	possīs	eās	velīs	ferās	fīās
sit	possit	eat	velit	ferat	fīat
sīmus	possīmus	eāmus	velīmus	ferāmus	fīāmus
sītis	possītis	eātis	velītis	ferātis	fīātis
sint	possint	eant	velint	ferant	fīant

IMPERFECT SUBJUNCTIVE

essem*	possem	īrem	vellem	ferrem	fierem
essēs	possēs	īrēs	vellēs	ferrēs	fierēs
esset	posset	īret	vellet	ferret	fieret
essēmus	possēmus	īrēmus	vellēmus	ferrēmus	fierēmus
essētis	possētis	īrētis	vellētis	ferrētis	fierētis
essent	possent	īrent	vellent	ferrent	fierent

PERFECT SUBJUNCTIVE

fuerim	potuerim	ierim[§]	voluerim	tulerim	†
fuerīs	potuerīs	ierīs[§]	voluerīs	tulerīs	
etc.	*etc.*	*etc.*	*etc.*	*etc.*	

PLUPERFECT SUBJUNCTIVE

fuissem	potuissem	iissem[§]	voluissem	tulissem	†
fuissēs	potuissēs	iissēs[§]	voluissēs	tulissēs	
etc.	*etc.*	*etc.*	*etc.*	*etc.*	

* Sometimes *forem, forēs*, etc.

§ Sometimes *īverim, īverīs, īvissem, īvissēs*, etc.

† For these tenses, passive forms of *faciō* are used, e.g. *factus sim*.

3 *Other forms*

IMPERATIVE SINGULAR AND PLURAL

es, este	–	ī, īte	–	fer, ferte	fī, fīte

PRESENT PARTICIPLE

–*	potēns**	iēns§	volēns	ferēns	–

FUTURE PARTICIPLE

futūrus	–	itūrus	–	lātūrus	–

PRESENT INFINITIVE

esse	posse	īre	velle	ferre	fierī

PERFECT INFINITIVE

fuisse	potuisse	iisse	voluisse	tulisse	†

FUTURE INFINITIVE

{ futūrus esse	–	itūrus esse	–	lātūrus esse	†
sometimes fore					

GERUND

–	–	eundum	volendum	ferendum	–

SUPINE

–	–	itum	–	lātum	–

For passive forms of *ferō*, see paragraph 5.

4 The forms of *fīō* are used as present, future and imperfect tenses of the passive of *faciō* 'I make', 'I do', etc.

servī nihil faciunt.	nihil **fit**.
The slaves are doing nothing.	Nothing is being done.
	or, Nothing is happening.
populus mē rēgem faciet.	rēx **fīam**.
The people will make me king.	I shall be made king.
	or, I shall become king.

The other tenses of the passive of *faciō* are formed in the usual way:

equitēs impetum fēcērunt.	impetus ab equitibus **factus est**.
The cavalry made an attack.	An attack was made by the cavalry.

* *sum* has no present participle, but compounds of *sum*, such as *absum*, *praesum* and the other verbs listed in **34**.6e, have present participles ending in *-ēns*, e.g. *absēns* 'being away', *praesēns* 'being in charge'.

** *potēns* is used as an adjective, meaning 'powerful'.

§ The present participle of *eō* is very rarely met, but compounds of *eō*, such as *exeō*, *redeō* and the other verbs listed in **34**.6a, have present participles ending in *-iēns* (genitive *-euntis*), e.g. *exiēns* (genitive *exeuntis*) 'going out', *rediēns* (genitive *redeuntis*) 'returning'.

† For these forms, the passive of *faciō* is used, e.g. *factus esse* 'to have been made, to have become'.

5 **ferō** has the following passive forms:

Indicative	Subjunctive
PRESENT *('I am brought')*	PRESENT
feror	ferar
fereris*	ferāris
fertur	*etc.*
ferimur	
feriminī	
feruntur	
FUTURE *('I shall be brought')*	
ferar	
ferēris	
etc.	
IMPERFECT *('I was being brought')*	IMPERFECT
ferēbar	ferrer
ferēbāris	ferrēris
etc.	*etc.*
PERFECT *('I have been brought, I was brought')*	PERFECT
lātus sum	lātus sim
lātus es	lātus sīs
etc.	*etc.*
FUTURE PERFECT *('I shall have been brought')*	
lātus erō	
lātus eris	
etc.	
PLUPERFECT *('I had been brought')*	PLUPERFECT
lātus eram	lātus essem
lātus erās	lātus essēs
etc.	*etc.*

Other forms	
IMPERATIVE *('be carried!')*	PRESENT PASSIVE INFINITIVE *('to be brought')*
singular ferre	
plural feriminī	ferrī
PERFECT PASSIVE PARTICIPLE *('having been brought')*	PERFECT PASSIVE INFINITIVE *('to have been brought')*
lātus	lātus esse
GERUNDIVE *('being brought, needing to be brought')*	FUTURE PASSIVE INFINITIVE *('to be about to be brought')*
ferendus	lātum īrī

*fereris is very rarely met. An alternative form, *ferris*, is even rarer.

6 **nōlō** (= *nōn volō*, meaning 'I do not want, I refuse') and **mālō**
(= *magis volō*, meaning 'I prefer') have the following irregular forms:

PRESENT INDICATIVE		PRESENT SUBJUNCTIVE	
nōlō	mālō	nōlim	mālim
nōn vīs	māvīs	nōlīs	mālīs
nōn vult	māvult	*etc.*	*etc.*
nōlumus	mālumus		
nōn vultis	māvultis	IMPERFECT SUBJUNCTIVE	
nōlunt	mālunt	nōllem	māllem
		nōllēs	māllēs
PRESENT INFINITIVE		*etc.*	*etc.*
nōlle	mālle		

IMPERATIVE SINGULAR AND PLURAL	
nōlī, nōlīte	—

> For examples of *nōlī* and *nōlīte* used with the infinitive to order somebody
> not to do something, see **12**.2 and **21**.2.

7 **ōdī** 'I hate, I dislike' and **meminī** 'I remember' have three tenses, whose
meanings are present, future and past, but whose endings are formed
like the perfect, future perfect and pluperfect of ordinary verbs:

INDICATIVE

ōdī	I hate	ōderō	I shall hate	ōderam	I hated
ōdistī	you hate	ōderis	you will hate	ōderās	you hated
etc.		*etc.*		*etc.*	

meminī	I remember	meminerō	I shall remember	memineram	I remembered
meministī	you remember	memineris	you will remember	minerās	you remembered
etc.		*etc.*		*etc.*	

INFINITIVE	IMPERATIVE SINGULAR & PLURAL	SUBJUNCTIVE	
ōdisse to hate	—	ōderim ōderīs *etc.*	ōdissem ōdissēs *etc.*
meminisse to remember	mementō, mementōte remember!	meminerim meminerīs *etc.*	meminissem meminissēs *etc.*

8 *Exercise*   With the help of paragraphs 1–7, translate:

1 potest.

2 ferimus.

3 ībunt.

4 volēbātis.

5 fuistī.

6 fīēbant.

7 tulī.

8 lātus es.

9 nōlumus.

10 memineram.

In paragraphs 1–7, find the Latin for:

11 You (s.) are.

12 We go.

13 He becomes.

14 You (pl.) want.

15 We were going.

16 They were able.

17 I had been able.

With the help of paragraphs 1–7, work out the Latin for:

18 He has been.

19 You (pl.) were being brought.

20 They prefer (subjunctive).

PART TWO

SYNTAX
(formation of sentences)

10 Statements

1 currimus.   We run.
   puerī dormiunt.   The boys are asleep.
   nōn manēbit.   He (or she or it) will not stay.
   spectātōrēs plausērunt, flōrēsque   The spectators clapped and started
     iactāre coepērunt.   to throw flowers.

> Statements like those above are sometimes described as *direct* statements. For *indirect* statements, see **25**.4.

11 Questions

1 *introduced by a question-word*, such as *quis? quid? cūr? ubi?* etc.:

   quid facitis?   What are you doing?
   ubi sunt leōnēs?   Where are the lions?
   cūr regrediēbantur?   Why were they going back?

2 *with -ne*, added to the first word of the clause or sentence:

   audīvistīne strepitum?   Did you hear the din?
   līberābiturne captīvus?   Will the prisoner be freed?

3 *expressed by tone of voice*, indicated in writing by a question-mark:

   cibum habēs?   Have you got food?

4 *with **utrum** (sometimes omitted) followed by **an** . . . ? or **annōn?***, to express alternatives:

   utrum tē laudāvit an pūnīvit?   Did he praise you or punish you?
   utrum adhūc vīvit annōn?   Is he still alive or not?
   canem an fēlem ēmistis?   Did you buy a dog or a cat?

5 *introduced by* **nōnne**. . . ?, to suggest that the answer to the question will be 'yes':

nōnne eum vīdistis?	Surely you saw him? *or*, You saw him, didn't you?
nōnne rēx in aulā habitat?	Surely the king lives in a palace? *or*, The king lives in a palace, doesn't he?

6 *introduced by* **num**. . . ?, to suggest that the answer to the question will be 'no':

num servus es?	Surely you aren't a slave? *or*, You're not a slave, are you?

7 *with a subjunctive form of the verb*, indicating that the speaker is wondering what to do (*deliberative question*):

ubi gemmās cēlem?	Where am I to hide the jewels?
quōs deōs precēmur?	Which gods are we to pray to?
utrum maneam an abeam?	Am I to stay or go away?
ānulum reddāmus an retineāmus?	Should we give the ring back or keep it?

8 Further examples:

1 labōrantne servī?
2 īnsānus es an scelestus?
3 nōnne puerī dormiēbant?
4 quis tē sequēbātur?
5 epistulam meam accēpistis?
6 quandō advēnit nūntius?
7 utrum aquam an vīnum bibitis?
8 num oppidum captum est?
9 cūr illum librum legis?
10 fugiāmus an resistāmus?

Questions like those in paragraphs 1–6 are sometimes described as *direct* questions, and those in paragraph 7 as *direct deliberative* questions. For *indirect* questions and *indirect deliberative* questions, see **25**.2.

12 Commands

1 *with an imperative form of the verb*, giving an order to somebody:

trāde pecūniam!	Hand over the money!
respondēte!	Answer!
intrā!	Come in!
mē sequiminī!	Follow me!
cōnāre!	Try!

2 *with nōlī (plural nōlīte) and an infinitive*, ordering somebody NOT to do something:

nōlī dormīre!	Be unwilling to sleep! *or*, in more natural English: Don't sleep!
nōlīte mē dēserere!	Don't desert me!
nōlī respicere!	Don't look back!

3 *with a verb in the present tense of the subjunctive*, giving an order in the 1st person plural (and so including oneself in the order), or in the 3rd person singular or plural (and so giving an order *about* someone or something); this is known as the *jussive* use of the subjunctive:

vīllam ingrediāmur.	Let us go into the villa.
dīligentius labōrent.	Let them work harder. *or*, in more natural English: They are to work harder.
vīvāmus atque amēmus.	Let us live and love.

nē with the jussive subjunctive indicates that an order in the 1st or 3rd person is *negative*:

nē dēspērēmus!	Let us not despair!
nē haesitet dominus.	Let the master not hesitate. *or*, The master is not to hesitate.

> The jussive subjunctive is sometimes used in a 2nd-person form ('you') to indicate a mild command or piece of general advice:
> | | |
> |---|---|
> | hūc reveniās. | You are to come back here. |
> | parentibus pāreās. | You should obey your parents. |

4 Further examples:

1 accipe hanc pecūniam!	6 statim respondeāmus.
2 nōlīte currere!	7 nē in forō pugnēmus.
3 tacēte!	8 nūntius hodiē proficīscātur.
4 cavē canem!	9 loquere!
5 nōlī fundum vēndere!	10 cōnāminī!

5 > Commands like those above are sometimes described as *direct* commands. For *indirect* commands, see **25**.3.

13 Wishes

1   with **utinam** and the pluperfect subjunctive, indicating a wish about the
    PAST (adding nē if the wish is negative):

      utinam resistere potuissem!   If only I had been able to resist!
                                        or, I wish I had been able to resist!

      utinam nē reversī essent!   If only they had not turned back!

2   with **utinam** and the imperfect subjunctive, indicating a wish about the
    PRESENT (negative nē):

      utinam nē in hōc carcere   I wish we weren't shut up in this
        clauderēmur!   prison!

      utinam adesset!   If only he were here!
                                    or, I wish he were here!

3   with the present subjunctive (with or without **utinam**), indicating a wish
    about the FUTURE (negative nē):

      utinam effugiant!   May they escape!
                                    or, If only they escape!

      vīvat rēx!   May the king live!
                                    or, Long live the king!

14 Common uses of the cases

1   nominative:

1a indicating the subject* of a verb:
    poēta recitābat.   The poet was reciting.

1b indicating a complement (see footnote to **18**.1b):
    Valerius est **senex**.   Valerius is an old man.

2   vocative, indicating a person or thing being spoken to:

      cavē, **domine**!   Look out, master!
      quid accidit, **Publī**?   What happened, Publius?

---

*The subject of an active verb is the person (thing, people) who does the
action; the subject of a passive verb is the person (thing, people) to whom the
action is done.

3 *accusative*

3a indicating the *object* (or *direct object*) of an active verb (i.e. the person or thing to whom the action is done):

amīcōs prōdidistī. You betrayed your friends.

3b indicating how long something goes on:

multās hōrās iter faciēbam. I was travelling for many hours.

(Compare 6d; and for further examples, see **15**.1a.)

3c with certain prepositions:

per **aquam** through the water

in **urbem** into the city

(Compare 6e; and for further examples, see **15**.2a and **16**.1 and 3.)

3d in indirect statements:

scio **hominem** dormīre. I know the man to be asleep.
or, in more natural English:
I know that the man is asleep.

(For further examples, see **25**.4.)

3e in measurements:

mūrus **ducentōs pedēs** a wall 200 feet high
altus

3f in certain nouns and place-names, indicating a place to which there is movement:

rūs to the country

Dēvam to Chester

(For further examples, see **15**.2d(i).)

4 *genitive*

4a like 'of' in English, indicating possession:

gladiī **sociōrum meōrum** the swords of my companions

4b indicating the whole of something, of which a part or quantity has been mentioned:

parum **cibī** too small a quantity of food
or, in more natural English:
too little food

4c in description, especially of non-physical qualities:

eques **summae audāciae** a horseman of the utmost boldness
or, in more natural English:
a very bold horseman

(Compare 6b.)

4d with certain verbs* and adjectives†:
    patriae oblivīscar.   I shall forget my country.
    perītus **bellī**   having experience of war
                                   or, expert in warfare

4e indicating the value placed on something:
    honōrēs **parvī** aestimō.   I consider honours of little value.
                                    or, in more natural English:
                                    I care little for honours.

(Compare 6j.)

Further examples:

1 castra hostium
2 vir sexāgintā annōrum
3 immemor perīculī
4 satis pecūniae

5 *dative*

5a like 'to' in English, indicating the *indirect object* of a verb (i.e. a person or thing involved in the action, other than the subject or direct object):
    uxōrī pecūniam reddidī.   I returned the money to my wife.

5b with certain verbs§ and adjectives‡:
    lēgibus pārēmus.   We are obedient to the laws.
                                    or, We obey the laws.
    populō cārus erat.   He was dear to the people.
                                    or, He was loved by the people.

Continued

---

* e.g. *meminī* 'I remember'; *misereor* 'I pity'; *oblivīscor* 'I forget', and the five impersonal verbs listed in **19**.1c.

† e.g. *avidus* 'greedy (for)'; *cupidus* 'eager (for)'; *ignārus* 'unaware (of)'; *memor* 'mindful (of), remembering' and *immemor* 'forgetful (of)'; *perītus* 'skilful (in), experienced (in)'; *plēnus* 'full (of)'; *similis* 'like' and *dissimilis* 'unlike'. (*plēnus* can also be used with the ablative; *similis* and *dissimilis* can also be used with the dative.)

§ see examples listed in **35**.

‡ e.g. *cārus* 'dear (to)'; *fidēlis* 'faithful (to)'; *grātus* 'pleasing (to), acceptable (to)'; *iūcundus* 'delightful (to), pleasing (to)'; *similis* 'similar (to), like' and *dissimilis* 'dissimilar (to), unlike'; *ūtilis* 'useful (to)'. (*similis* and *dissimilis* can also be used with the genitive.)

5c in certain phrases with forms of the verb *sum* 'I am'* (this is known as the *predicative* use of the dative):

faber **magnō auxiliō** erit.	The workman will be a great help.
rēgēs omnibus **odiō** erant.	The kings were hateful to everybody. *or*, Everybody hated the kings.
dignitās tua mihi **cūrae** est.	Your dignity is a matter of concern to me.

5d indicating the person for whose advantage or disadvantage something is done:

servus **nōbīs** iānuam aperuit.	The slave opened the door for us.
fūrēs **mihi** omnia abstulērunt.	The thieves stole everything from me.

5e with a nominative and forms of *est* 'there is', indicating possession:

est **tibi** magna vīlla.	There is a large villa (belonging) to you. *or*, in more natural English: You have a large villa.
erat **nōbīs** nūlla spēs.	We had no hope.
sunt **mercātōrī** multae gemmae.	The merchant has many jewels.
cōnsulēs, **quibus** est summa potestās	the consuls, who have supreme power

5f with the gerundive, indicating the person by whom something has to be done:

mīlitibus plaustrum reficiendum erat.	For the soldiers, there was a wagon needing to be repaired. *or*, in more natural English: The soldiers had to repair a wagon.

(For further examples, see **26**.2b.)

Further examples:

1 iuvenis patrī aurum trādidit.
2 captīvīs parcere nōlō.
3 ille centuriō mīlitibus odiō est.
4 est mihi nāvis ingēns.
5 ancilla hospitibus vīnum effundēbat.
6 medicō cōnfīdimus
7 latrō mercātōrī dēnāriōs ēripuit.
8 templum nōbīs aedificandum est.

---

*e.g.

auxiliō esse	to be a help
cūrae esse	to be a cause for anxiety
dolōrī esse	to be a cause for grief
exemplō esse	to be an example
exitiō esse	to be a cause of destruction
honōrī esse	to be an honour
impedimentō esse	to be a hindrance
odiō esse	to be hateful
salūtī esse	to be a means of safety
ūsuī esse	to be useful

ablative

6a like 'by' or 'with' in English, indicating the method or instrument
by which something is done:*

clāmōribus excitātus   awakened by the shouts
hastīs armātī   armed with spears

6b in description, especially of physical qualities:
homō **vultū sevērō**   a man with a stern expression
▍ (Compare 4c.)

6c like English 'from', indicating the origin of someone or something:
clārā gente nātus   born from a famous family

6d indicating the time at which (or within which) something happens:
tertiō mēnse revēnit.   He returned in the third month.
▍ (Compare 3b; and for further examples, see **15.1b**.)

6e with certain prepositions:
ex **hortīs**   out of the gardens
in **Britanniā**   in Britain
▍ (Compare 3c; and for further examples, see **15.2b** and c and **16.2** and 3.)

6f in comparisons:
perītior **frātre** sum.   I am more skilful than my brother.
▍ (A commoner way of expressing the same idea is *perītior sum quam frāter*.)

6g with certain verbs† and adjectives§:
dignus **suppliciō**   worthy of punishment
nāvibus ūtēbantur.   They were using ships.
cibō carēmus.   We are without food.

6h in certain nouns and place-names, indicating a place from which
there is movement:
domō   from home
Pompēiīs   from Pompeii
▍ (For further examples, see **15.2d(ii)**.)

6j indicating the price at which something is bought or sold:
equum **vīlī pretiō** ēmī.   I bought the horse at a cheap price.
▍ (Compare 4e.)

Continued

---

  * The preposition *ā, ab* is used with the ablative to indicate a *person* by whom
    something is done:
    ab amīcīs excitātus   awakened by friends
    ā duce armātī   armed by the leader
    If the action is done by an *animal*, *ā, ab* may be either included or left out:
    cane excitātus = ā cane excitātus   awakened by the dog

  †e.g. *careō* 'I am without, I lack'; and the deponent verbs *fruor* 'I enjoy'; *fungor*
    'I carry out, I perform'; *ūtor* 'I use'; *vēscor* 'I feed (on)'.

  §e.g. *contentus* 'satisfied (with)'; *dignus* 'worthy (of)' and *indignus* 'unworthy
    (of)'; *frētus* 'relying (on)'; *plēnus* 'full (of)'; *vacuus* 'free (from)'. (*plēnus* can
    also be used with the genitive.)

6k indicating the extent by which two things differ from each other:

Marcus **multō** stultior est quam Sextus.	Marcus is much more stupid than Sextus.

6m in *ablative absolute* phrases made up of (i) a noun or pronoun, and (ii) an adjective, participle or second noun, grammatically disconnected from the rest of the sentence:

Caesare duce, mīlitēs urbem cēpērunt.	With Caesar as leader, the soldiers captured the city.
	or, in more natural English:
	Under Caesar's leadership, the soldiers captured the city.
Pompēiō Crassōque cōnsulibus, rēs dīra accidit.	With Pompey and Crassus being consuls, a terrible thing happened.
	or, in more natural English:
	In the consulship of Pompey and Crassus, a terrible thing happened.
mē invītō, fīlius abiit.	With me unwilling, my son went away.
	or, in more natural English:
	My son went away against my wishes.
nāve refectā, mercātor profectus est.	With the ship having been repaired, the merchant set out.
	or, in more natural English:
	When the ship had been repaired, the merchant set out.

(For more examples of ablative absolute phrases containing participles, see **20**.7.)

Further examples:

1 servus, vulnere impedītus, currere nōn poterat.
2 pictūram decem dēnāriīs vēndidī.
3 senex ingentī corpore prope iānuam stābat.
4 sextō diē nūntius ad vīllam vēnit.
5 haec puella multō callidior omnibus sorōribus est.
6 Boudiccā rēgīnā, Britannī rebelliōnem contrā Rōmānōs fēcērunt.
7 tōtum templum flammīs cōnsūmptum est.
8 amīcus noster summā laude dignus erat.
9 tē duce, hostēs facile vincēmus!
10 Marcus, auxiliō amīcōrum ūsus, domum novam celeriter aedificāvit.

7 For an exercise practising the uses and forms of the different cases, see **1**.7.

8 For examples of the use of the *locative* case, see **15**.2d(iii).

15 Time and place

1 *time*

1a The *accusative* case (with or without *per*), indicates HOW LONG an action goes on:

duās hōrās latēbam.	I lay hidden for two hours.
quīnque diēs nāvigābant.	They were sailing for five days.

1b The *ablative* case indicates WHEN something happens:

sextā hōrā profectī sunt.	They set off at the sixth hour.
quārtō annō bellī rēx mortuus est.	In the fourth year of the war, the king died.

Further examples:

1 per tōtam noctem pugnāvimus.

2 quīntō diē amīcus advēnit.

3 octō annōs senex in urbe habitābat.

4 secundā hōrā ē lectō surrēxī.

1c The *ablative* case is also used to indicate the time WITHIN WHICH something happens:

tribus mēnsibus revēnī.	I came back within three months.

2 *place*

2a ***in*** or ***ad*** *with the accusative case** indicates the place TO which there is movement:

ad urbem	to the city	in Graeciam†	to Greece
ad Ītaliam	to Italy†	ad forum	to the forum

2b ***ā, ab*** *or* ***ē, ex*** *with the ablative case** indicates the place FROM which there is movement:

ex oppidō	from/out of the town	ab Āfricā	from Africa
ē Britanniā	from/out of Britain	ā lītore	from the seashore

2c ***in*** *with the ablative case** indicates the place WHERE something happens:

in Graeciā	in Greece	in Galliā	in Gaul
in templō	in the temple	in viīs	in the streets

Continued

---

* In verse, the prepositions *in, ad, ā, ab, ē, ex* are sometimes omitted:

terram Hesperiam veniēs.	You will come to a land in the west.
exarsit dolor **ossibus**.	Grief flared up in his bones.
proficīscitur **urbe**.	He is setting out from the city.

†*ad Ītaliam iit* means 'he went (as far as but not in)to Italy'; *in Graeciam iit* means 'he went (in)to Greece'.

2d If the place-name is the name of a town or small island,* or is one of the nouns *domus, humus, rūs,*

(i) the *accusative* case (without *ad* or *in*) indicates the place to which there is movement:

Dēvam	to Chester	domum	home, homewards
Pompēiōs	to Pompeii	rūs	to the country

(ii) the *ablative* case (without *ē, ex* or *ā, ab*) indicates the place from which there is movement:

Rōmā	from Rome	domō	from home
Athēnīs	from Athens	rūre	from the country

(iii) the *locative* case (whose formation is shown in **1**.10) indicates the place where something happens:

Alexandrīae	in/at Alexandria	domī	at home
Eborācī	in/at York	rūrī	in the country
Pompēiīs	in/at Pompeii	humī	on the ground

Further examples:

1 nēmō in forō erat; nam omnēs cīvēs ad amphitheātrum festīnābant.
2 mercātōrēs, ex Ītaliā profectī, in Siciliā duōs mēnsēs mānsērunt.
3 pater tuus heri rūre abiit, ut pompam Rōmae spectāret.
4 hodiē domī labōrō; crās tamen iter Athēnās faciam.
5 nūntiī prīmā lūce Pompēiīs discessērunt et Rōmam contendērunt.
6 centuriō, Dēvae in pugnā vulnerātus, in Galliam redīre temptāvit; Londiniī autem mortuus est.

---

* i.e. an island small enough to be regarded as a single 'place', or containing no more than one town.

16 Common prepositions

1 *used with the accusative case*

ad	to, towards
ante	before
apud	at the house of; among
circum	around
contrā	against
extrā	outside
inter	among, between
intrā	inside
per	through
post	after, behind
praeter	past; except
prope	near
propter	on account of, because of
trāns	across
ultrā	beyond

2 *used with the ablative case*

ā, ab	from; by
cum	with
dē	down from; about
ē, ex	out of
prō	in front of; on behalf of
sine	without

3 *used sometimes with the accusative, sometimes with the ablative*

in	(with accusative) into; (with ablative) in
super	over
sub	under

These prepositions are used with the accusative if movement is involved; otherwise with the ablative:

in forō ambulābat.	She was walking in the forum.
in forum ruit.	She rushed into the forum.
super mēnsam saluit.	He jumped over the table.
sub mēnsā iacēbat.	He was lying under the table.

17 Agreement

1 *agreement (in number) between nominative noun and verb*
    servus slave   servus **labōrat**.   The slave works.
servus is singular; so the verb *labōrat* is also singular.

    servī slaves   servī **labōrant**.   The slaves work.
servī is plural; so the verb *labōrant* is also plural.

2 *agreement (in case, gender and number) between noun and adjective*
    captīvus **puellae** crēdidit.   The prisoner trusted the girl.
    captīvus puellae **benignae** crēdidit. The prisoner trusted the kindly girl.
puellae is dative, feminine and singular; so *benignae*, which describes
puellae, is also dative, feminine and singular.
    mīlitēs vīdī.   I saw the soldiers.
    mīlitēs **ignāvōs** vīdī.   I saw the lazy soldiers.
mīlitēs is accusative, masculine and plural; so *ignāvōs*, which describes
mīlitēs, is also accusative, masculine and plural.

> For an exercise practising agreement between noun and adjective, see **2.6**.

3 *agreement (in case) between one noun (or noun + adjective phrase) and another*
    Marcus surrēxit.   Marcus stood up.
    Marcus **centuriō** surrēxit.   Marcus the centurion stood up.
Marcus is nominative; so the noun *centuriō*, which describes *Marcus*, is
also nominative. (This is sometimes described as *apposition*; *centuriō* is
said to be 'in apposition' to *Marcus*.)
    fūr **Sextum** fallere nōn potuit.   The thief could not fool Sextus.
    fūr Sextum, **virum callidum**,   The thief could not fool Sextus,
       fallere nōn potuit.   a cunning man.
Sextum is accusative; so the phrase *virum callidum*, which is in
apposition to *Sextum*, is also accusative.

4 *agreement (in gender and number) between noun (or pronoun) and relative
pronoun* (whose forms are shown in **5.7**)
    ancillae . . . cantābant.   The slave-girls were singing.
    ancillae, **quae** in culīnā   The slave-girls, who were working
       labōrābant, cantābant.   in the kitchen, were singing.
ancillae is feminine plural; so *quae*, which refers to *ancillae*, is also
feminine plural (*ancillae* is described as the *antecedent* of *quae*).
    puer . . . rīsit.   The boy smiled.
    puer **cui** dōnum dedī rīsit.   The boy to whom I gave a present smiled.
puer is masculine singular; so *cui*, which refers to *puer*, is also masculine
singular (*puer* is the antecedent of *cui*).

The *gender* and *number* of a relative pronoun are fixed by its antecedent,
as described above. But the *case* of a relative pronoun is fixed by the way
it fits into the relative clause. For instance, in the first example above,
quae is the subject of *labōrābant*, and is therefore nominative; in the second
example, *cui* is the indirect object of *dedī*, and is therefore dative.

Further examples:

1 puella, quae in cubiculō dormiēbat, nihil audīvit.
2 hic est gladius quō rēx occīsus est.
3 gemmae, quās mercātor in Āfricā ēmerat, pretiōsissimae erant.
4 templum, quod in mediō oppidō stābat, saepe vīsitābam.
5 ubi sunt clientēs quibus heri cibum dedimus?
6 senex cuius pecūniam puerī invēnerant grātiās maximās eīs ēgit.

In each example, pick out the antecedent, and explain the gender, number and case of the relative pronoun.

18 Attributive and predicative uses of adjectives and nouns

attributive

1a **magnus** leō dormiēbat.
The large lion was asleep.

2a Sextus **victor** rīsit.
The victorious Sextus smiled.

3a mīles **mortuus** sepeliēbātur.
The dead soldier was being buried.

4a Publium **cōnsulem** cōnspexī.
I spotted the consul Publius.

5a āthlētam **fortissimum** spectābant.
They were watching a very brave athlete.

predicative

1b leō est **magnus**.*
The lion is large.

2b Sextus **victor** rediit.
Sextus came back victorious.

3b mīles **mortuus** prōcubuit.
The soldier fell down dead.

4b Publium **cōnsulem** creāvī.
I appointed Publius (as) consul.

5b āthlētam **fortissimum** putābant.
They thought the athlete very brave.

6 To decide whether an adjective (or noun) is being used attributively or predicatively, it is necessary to look at *the whole sentence*. For instance: In sentence 3a an attributive translation ('The dead soldier was being buried') would normally make better sense than a predicative one ('The soldier was being buried dead') unless the circumstances were rather peculiar, e.g. if the speaker were denying an accusation that he had buried the soldier alive.
Similarly, in sentence 4b a predicative translation ('I appointed Publius (as) consul') would normally make better sense than an attributive one ('I appointed the consul Publius').

7 Further examples:

1 in mediā pompā ambulābant septem captīvī. captīvus prīmus superbē circumspectābat; cēterī lacrimābant.
2 frāter tuus prīmus advēnit, ultimus discessit.
3 ubi Claudius appāruit, mīlitēs eum imperātōrem salūtāvērunt.
4 Claudius imperātor venēnō necātus est.

---

*A noun or adjective used predicatively with a form of *sum* 'I am' or of such verbs as *fīō* 'I become' or *videor* 'I seem' is sometimes described as a *complement*, because it *completes* the sense of the sentence. For example, *magnus* is the complement in sentence 1b.

19 Impersonal use of verbs

1 *3rd person singular active forms* (shown in heavy print):

1a *without a noun or pronoun*
    advesperāscit.   It is getting late.
    semper **pluēbat**.   It was always raining.
    tonuit.   It thundered.

1b *with a noun or pronoun in the accusative case* (shown in italics):
    decet *tē* deōs immortālēs honōrāre.
    It is proper that you honour the immortal gods.
    or, in more natural English:
    You ought to honour the immortal gods.

    Rōmānōs numquam **oportet** hostibus crēdere.
    It is never right that Romans trust the enemy.
    or, Romans must never trust the enemy.

1c *with a noun or pronoun in the accusative case* (indicating the person
    who feels an emotion, and shown here in italics) *and another in the
    genitive* (indicating the cause of the emotion):
    coquum stultitiae **pudēbat**.
    It made the cook ashamed of his stupidity.
    or, The cook was ashamed of his stupidity.

    puellam cibī vīnīque **taedet**.
    It makes the girl tired of food and wine.
    or, The girl is tired of food and wine.

    The five verbs used in this way are:
    miseret (mē)   it makes me feel pity, *or* I pity, I am sorry for
    paenitet (mē)   it makes me regret, *or* I regret, I am sorry about
    piget (mē)   it vexes me, *or* I am vexed at
    pudet (mē)   it makes me ashamed, *or* I am ashamed of
    taedet (mē)   it makes me tired, *or* I am tired of

1d *with a noun or pronoun in the dative case* (italicised):
    libet *mihi* hoc dōnum accipere.
    It is agreeable to me to receive this present.
    or, I am glad to receive this present.

    placuit *nōbīs* fugere.
    It pleased us to run away, *or* We decided to run away.

    iuvenibus iam **licet** redīre.
    It is now permitted to the young men to come back.
    or, The young men may now come back.

Further examples:

1 cotīdiē pluit.
2 semper oportet nōs fidem servāre.
3 patrī meō libet prope mare habitāre.
4 nōlīte intrāre! decet vōs extrā iānuam manēre.
5 rēgem crūdēlitātis nōn pudēbat.
6 nōn licuit mihi vīnum bibere.
7 mīlitibus placuit ā castrīs discēdere.
8 fūrem sceleris iam paenitet.

2 *3rd person singular passive forms*, used to indicate an action without indicating the doer of the action:

curritur.	It is being run. *or*, in more natural English: Running is taking place, a race is going on, etc.
pugnātum est.	It was fought. *or*, in more natural English: Fighting took place, a battle was fought, etc.
tibi parcētur.	Mercy will be shown to you. *or*, in more natural English: You will be shown mercy, you will be spared.

20 Uses of the participles

1 *present participle*

canis dominum **intrantem** vīdit.
The dog saw his master entering.

prīncipī ē Campāniā **redeuntī** complūrēs senātōrēs obviam iērunt.
Several senators went to meet the emperor returning from
   Campania.
or, When the emperor was returning from Campania, several
   senators went to meet him.

2   *perfect active participle* (deponent verbs only)

> senex, multās iniūriās **passus**, auxilium ā patrōnō petīvit.
> The old man, having suffered many acts of injustice, sought help
>   from his patron.

3   *perfect passive participle*

> fūrēs, ad iūdicem **ductī**, veniam petīvērunt.
> The thieves, having been led to the judge, begged for mercy.

> ānulum **inventum** ad centuriōnem attulimus.
> We brought the ring, having been found, to the centurion.
> *or*, in more natural English:
> When the ring had been found, we brought it to the centurion.

4   *future participle*

> mercātōrēs nāvem **cōnscēnsūrōs** vīdī.
> I saw the merchants about to go on board the ship.

5   Each of the participles in paragraphs 1–4 refers to a noun. For instance,
in the first example in paragraph 1, *intrantem* refers to *dominum*. A
participle agrees in case, gender and number with the noun it refers to;
in paragraph 1 *dominum* is accusative masculine singular, and so
intrantem is also accusative masculine singular.

6   Sometimes the noun or pronoun to which the participle refers is not
mentioned in the sentence:

> ingēns multitūdō **fugientium** viās omnēs complēvit.
> A huge crowd of (people) running away filled all the streets.

> ab amīcīs **incitātus**, in Circō Maximō certāvit.
> Having been urged on by his friends, he competed in the Circus
>   Maximus.

7   *participle used with noun or pronoun in ablative absolute phrase*,
grammatically disconnected from the rest of the sentence:

> **ānulō inventō**, omnēs gaudēbant.
> With the ring having been found, everyone was glad.
> *or*, in more natural English:
> When the ring had been found, everyone was glad.

> (If *ānulō inventō* were omitted from this example, the remaining words
> *omnēs gaudēbant* would still make a complete sentence. Compare the
> second example in paragraph 3, which would no longer make a complete
> sentence if *ānulum inventum* were omitted.)

> **duce loquente**, nūntius accurrit.
> With the leader speaking, a messenger came dashing up.
> *or*, While the leader was speaking, a messenger came dashing up.

dominā ēgressā, servī garrīre coepērunt.
With the mistress having gone out, the slaves began to chatter.
or, After the mistress had gone out, the slaves began to chatter.

mīlitibus īnstrūctīs, tuba sonuit.
With the soldiers having been drawn up, a trumpet sounded.
or, When the soldiers had been drawn up, a trumpet sounded.

> For examples of ablative absolute phrases containing adjectives and pairs of nouns, see **14**.6m.

8 *examples of different ways of translating participles*

forum ingressī, ...   Having entered the forum, ...
When they had entered the forum, ...
After entering the forum, ...
They entered the forum and . . . .
Because they had entered the forum, ...
Although they had entered the forum, ...
On entering the forum, ...
On their entry into the forum, they . . . .   *etc.*

in hortō labōrāns, ...   Working in the garden, ...
While working in the garden, ...
As he was working in the garden, ...
During his work in the garden, he . . . .   *etc.*

The most suitable way of translating a participle in any sentence depends on the sense of the sentence as a whole.

9 Further examples:

1 statuae deōrum, ex aurō factae, ad templum portābantur.
2 ponte dēlētō, nēmō flūmen trānsīre poterat.
3 ecce! duōs elephantōs videō per viam prōcēdentēs.
4 dux, mīlitēs hortātus, prīncipia intrāvit.
5 poētā recitante, fūr pecūniam spectātōribus auferēbat.
6 puer, pugnantium clāmōre perterritus, fūgit.
7 Rōmānī urbem captam incendērunt.
8 Rōmānī, urbe captā, valdē gaudēbant.
9 senex moritūrus fīliōs ad sē vocāvit.
10 iuvenem, hastā vulnerātum, ad medicum dūximus.
11 amīcō ex Ītaliā discēdentī centum dēnāriōs dedī.
12 ab Imperātōre ipsō laudāta, rīsit.

Pick out the participle in each sentence, and identify the noun (if any) that it describes. Which sentences contain ablative absolute phrases?

10 > For examples of different types of word order in sentences containing participles, see **28**.2 and 3.

21 Uses of the infinitives*

1   *with verbs such as **possum** 'I am able', **volō** 'I want', **dēbeō** 'I must', **timeō** 'I am afraid', etc.:*

crās **proficīscī** volō.	I want to set off tomorrow.
senex **festīnāre** nōn poterat.	The old man was unable to hurry. *or*, The old man could not hurry.
iuvenis **respondēre** timēbat.†	The young man was afraid to reply.

2   *with **nōlī**, **nōlīte**, ordering somebody not to do something (as described in **12**.2):*

nōlī mē **culpāre**!	Don't put the blame on me!
nōlīte hīc **manēre**!	Don't stay here!

3   *with phrases such as **decōrum est**, **difficile est**, etc.:*

difficile mihi erit aequō animō **loquī**.	It will be difficult for me to speak calmly.

4   *with impersonal verbs such as **placet**, **licet**, etc. (**19**.1):*

līberīs **exīre** nōn licuit.	The children were not allowed to go out.

5   *with **iubeō** 'I order' and **vetō** 'I forbid, I order. . . not' (**25**.3):*

rēx nōs **comprehendī** iussit.	The king ordered us to be arrested.
mercātor nautās vīnum **bibere** vetuit.	The merchant told the sailors not to drink the wine.

6   *as a 'historic' infinitive, indicating one or more actions in the past, usually in vivid or quickly-moving narrative:*

tum dēmum omnēs **dēspērāre**; in viās **ruere**, **clāmāre**, hūc illūc **currere**.
Then at last they were all in despair; they were rushing into the streets, shouting and running this way and that.

---

* For further examples of some of these uses, see the paragraph referred to under each sub-heading.

†For examples of another way of using verbs meaning 'I am afraid', see **23**.8.

7   *to express indirect statements* (**25**.4):

> hospitēs ançillam optimē **cantāvisse** putāvērunt.
> The guests thought that the slave-girl had sung excellently.

> crēdō mīlitēs fidem **servātūrōs esse**.
> I believe that the soldiers will keep their word.

8   Further examples:

1 facile erat sacerdōtibus vērum cognōscere.
2 nōn licet vōbīs in viā lūdere.
3 nōlī mē tangere!
4 nāvem reficere tandem poterāmus.
5 centuriō audīvit omnēs captīvōs effūgisse.
6 pecūniam patrī reddere dēbēs.
7 dux epistulam statim scrībī iussit.
8 spectātōrēs īrātissimī erant. exclāmāre; gladiātōrem vituperāre; etiam lapidēs iacere; tōtum amphitheātrum strepitū complērī.

22 Main clauses and subordinate clauses

1   *sentences consisting of a main clause only*

  cīvēs conveniēbant.   The citizens were gathering.
  senex medicum arcessīvit. The old man sent for the doctor.

2   *sentences consisting of a main clause and subordinate clause*

coquus numquam labōrat, **quod semper dormit**.
The cook never works, because he is always asleep.

haruspicēs, **cum victimās īnspexissent**, *ōmina nūntiāvērunt.*
The soothsayers, when they had inspected the victims, announced the omens.
or, After inspecting the victims, the soothsayers announced the omens.

Each of these sentences is made up of:

(i) a *main clause*, i.e. a group of words which would make a complete sentence on its own (*coquus numquam labōrat* in the first example, and *haruspicēs ōmina nūntiāvērunt* in the second);

(ii) a *subordinate clause*, i.e. a group of words introduced by a word like *quod* or *cum* (*quod semper dormit* in the first example, and *cum victimam īnspexissent* in the second). A subordinate clause on its own cannot make a complete sentence.

Further examples:

1 mercātor amīcōs ad cēnam invītāvit quod diem nātālem celebrābat.
2 iuvenis, simulac nōmen suum audīvit, surrēxit.
3 quamquam servī multum frūmentum in horreum intulerant, dominus nōn erat contentus.
4 tot vīllās habeō ut eās nūmerāre nōn possim.

In each sentence, pick out the main clause and subordinate clause.

3   A Latin sentence may contain more than one subordinate clause:

quamquam appropinquābant hostēs, *quī hastās vibrābant,* centuriō immōtus manēbat.
The centurion remained motionless, although the enemy were approaching, who were brandishing spears.

centuriō immōtus manēbat is the main clause; the other two groups of words are subordinate clauses.

4   For examples of different types of word order in sentences containing main clauses and subordinate clauses, see **28.1–4**.

23 Common types of subordinate clause

1 *relative clauses*, usually introduced by forms of the relative pronoun *quī* (shown in **5.**7) or relative adverbs such as *ubi*:

mīlitēs **quōs imperātor mīserat** in castrīs manēbant.
The soldiers whom the emperor had sent remained in the camp.
prope iānuam stābat nūntius, **cui epistulam trādidī**.
Near the door stood a messenger, to whom I handed the letter.
haec est domus **ubi lībertus meus habitat**.
This is the house where my freedman lives.

> For examples of agreement between antecedent and relative pronoun, see **17.**4.

Forms of *is* are often used as antecedents to forms of *quī*:

is quī illam fābulam nārrāvit mentiēbātur.
He who told that story was lying.
or, The man who told that story was lying.
eī quī fūgērunt mox capientur.
Those who ran away will soon be caught.
id quod nauta dīxit nōs maximē perturbāvit.
That which the sailor said alarmed us very much.
or, What the sailor said alarmed us very much.
eās vīllās vēndidī **quae** mē minimē dēlectābant.
I sold those villas that least appealed to me.

> For examples of sentences in which the antecedent comes after the relative clause or is omitted altogether, see **28.**1c.

Similar to the use of *is* with *quī* is the use of *tantus* with *quantus*, *tam* with *quam*, *tot* with *quot*, etc.:

fīlius meus **tam** fortis est **quam** leō.
My son is as brave as a lion.
tot agricolae aderant **quot** mīlitēs.
There were as many farmers present as soldiers.
tantum praemium tū accēpistī **quantum** ego.
You received as big a reward as I did.

Further examples:
1 ubi est liber quem herī legēbam?
2 puella quae adstābat senem salūtāvit.
3 captīvī quōs rēx ē carcere līberāverat maximās grātiās eī ēgērunt.
4 omnēs cīvēs imperātōrī, quī urbī iam appropinquābat, obviam iērunt.
5 id quod dīcis falsum est.
6 nihil est tam perīculōsum quam mare.

> For examples of a different way of using the relative pronoun (the *connecting* use), see **5.**7.

> For examples of forms of *quī* used with the subjunctive in purpose clauses and result clauses, see paragraphs 2 and 3 below.

2 *purpose clauses* (sometimes called *final* clauses), introduced by *ut, nē* or forms of *quī* or other relative words, followed by a subjunctive form of the verb in the present or imperfect tense:

imperātor ipse adest **ut fābulam spectet**.
The emperor himself is here in order that he may watch the play.
or, The emperor himself is here to watch the play.

mīlitēs ēmīsit **quī turbam dēpellerent**.
He sent out soldiers who were to drive the crowd away.
or, He sent out soldiers to drive the crowd away.

fēlēs arborem ascendit **nē ā puerīs caperētur**.
The cat climbed up a tree so that it should not be caught by the boys.
or, The cat climbed up a tree in order not to be caught by the boys.

Further examples:

1 fabrī tōtam noctem labōrāvērunt ut templum ante lūcem perficerent.
2 coquus aquam attulit quā flammae exstinguerentur.
3 dēsilite in hanc fossam, ut hastās hostium vītētis!
4 domum tacitī intrāvimus, nē ā cane audīrēmur.

> Purpose clauses containing the comparative form of an adjective or adverb are normally introduced by *quō*:
> nāvem condūxī, **quō celerius ad Ītaliam revenīrem**.
> I hired a ship, in order to return to Italy more quickly.

3 *result clauses* (sometimes called *consecutive* clauses), expressed by *ut** and a subjunctive form of the verb, usually in the present or imperfect tense:

tam perītus est faber **ut ab omnibus laudētur**.
The craftsman is so skilful that he is praised by everybody.

tanta erat nūbēs **ut pāstōrēs sōlem vidēre nōn possent**.
The cloud was so great that the shepherds could not see the sun.

When a main clause contains one of the following words, it often leads on to a result clause:

tam	so	tot	so many
tālis	such	adeō	so (= to such an extent)
tantus	so big, so great	ita, sīc	so (= in such a way)

---

* Some types of result clause are introduced by forms of *quī* (meaning 'of the sort who . . .', etc.):

nōn is est **quī terreātur**. He is not a person of the sort who is scared.
or, He is not such a man as to be scared.

erant **quī resisterent**. There were people of such a sort as to resist.
or, more naturally, Some people resisted.

Further examples:

1 tantus erat clāmor ut nēmō verba rēgis audīret.
2 gladiātor spectātōrēs adeō dēlectāvit ut iterum iterumque plauderent.
3 tam benignus es ut ab omnibus cīvibus amēris.
4 tot vulnera accēperam ut medicus dē vītā meā dēspērāret.

4 *causal clauses*, indicating a cause or reason, expressed by *quod* or *quia* 'because' and an indicative form of the verb, or by *cum* 'since' and a subjunctive:

> imperātor Agricolae invidēbat **quod multās rēs splendidās gesserat**.
> The emperor was jealous of Agricola because he had done many splendid deeds.

> asinus, **quia obstinātus erat**, prōgredī nōluit.
> The donkey, because it was obstinate, refused to go on.

> tibi, **cum amīcus sīs**, pecūniam meam mandābō.
> I shall entrust my money to you, since you are my friend.

quod and *quia* are also used with the *subjunctive* to quote a reason put forward by some other person or people, with whom the speaker may or may not happen to agree:

> Socratēs damnātus est quod iuvenēs **corrumperet**.
> Socrates was condemned because (according to his accusers) he corrupted young men.

>> (Compare this with a causal clause in which the *indicative* is used:
>>
>> Socratēs damnātus est quod iuvenēs **corrumpēbat**.
>> Socrates was condemned because (in fact) he corrupted young men.)

Further examples:

1 candidātō vestrō nōn faveō, quia mendāx est.
2 māter fīlium vituperāvit quod tardus ē lectō surrēxisset.
3 māter fīlium vituperāvit quod tardus ē lectō surrēxerat.

5   *temporal clauses*, indicating the time at which something happens, introduced by such words as:

> ubi 'when' (followed by an indicative form of the verb)
> postquam 'after'   „
> simulac, simulatque 'as soon as'   „
> antequam, priusquam 'before'   „
> dōnec 'until'   „
> dum 'until, while'   „
> cum 'when' (followed by a subjunctive in the imperfect or
>   pluperfect tense)

simulac rēx ātrium intrāvit, omnēs surrēxērunt.
As soon as the king came into the hall, everybody stood up.

in tabernā vīnum bibēbam **dōnec uxor caupōnis mē ēiēcit**.
I was drinking wine in the inn until the innkeeper's wife threw me out.

mercātōrēs, **cum cōnsilium audīvissent**, libenter cōnsēnsērunt.
When the merchants had heard the plan, they willingly agreed.

> *antequam* and *priusquam* are sometimes split into separate words, *ante . . . quam* and *prius . . . quam*:
> > nūntiī **ante** discessērunt **quam sōl ortus est**.
> > The messengers left before the sun rose.
>
> A Latin perfect tense after *postquam*, *simulac* or *ubi* is often translated by an English pluperfect:
> > dominus, **postquam fundum īnspexit**, ad urbem rediit.
> > After the master had inspected the farm, he went back to the city.

priusquam, *dum* and *dōnec* are used with the subjunctive to add the idea of purpose to the idea of time:

exspectābant **dum sacerdōs signum daret**.
They were waiting until the priest should give the signal.
or, They were waiting for the priest to give the signal.

fugiendum est nōbīs **priusquam custōdēs nōs cōnspiciant**.
We must run away before the guards catch sight of us.

dum meaning 'while' (i.e. 'at one point during the time that . . .') is used with a present tense even if the sentence refers to past time:

dum bellum in Britanniā geritur, rēs dīra Rōmae accidit.
While the war was being waged in Britain, a terrible disaster happened at Rome.

Further examples:

1 hospitēs, ubi cibum gustāvērunt, coquum valdē laudāvērunt.
2 centuriō, cum fenestram frāctam cōnspexisset, vehementer saeviēbat.
3 cīvēs, simulatque ad apodytērium revēnērunt, vestīmenta induērunt.
4 rēx, postquam epistulam servō dictāvit, nūntium arcessīvit.
5 fūr, priusquam caperētur, ē vīllā ruit.
6 dum pāstor dormit, lupī duōs agnōs rapuērunt.

> *cum* 'when' is used with an *indicative* form of the verb to introduce the following four types of temporal clause:
>
> (i) *referring to present or future time*
>
> **cum sorōrem tuam vīderō**, epistulam eī referam.
> When I see your sister, I shall deliver the letter to her.
>
> (ii) *placed after the main clause and indicating the chief event of the sentence*
>
> paene domum pervēnerat, **cum subitō latrōnēs ex īnsidiīs ērūpērunt**.
> He had almost reached home, when suddenly robbers burst out from
>   an ambush.
>
> (iii) *strongly emphasising the idea of time*
>
> **cum tū in lectō dormiēbās**, eō tempore nōs in agrīs labōrābāmus.
> At the time when you were asleep in bed, we were toiling in the fields.
>
> (iv) *meaning 'whenever . . .'*, followed by a verb in the PLUPERFECT
> tense if the verb in the main clause is *past*, and by a verb in the PERFECT
> tense if the main verb is *present*:
>
> **cum puer errāverat**, magister eum pūniēbat.
> Whenever the boy made a mistake, the teacher used to punish him.
>
> **cum eum salūtāvī**, mē vituperat.
> Whenever I greet him, he is rude to me.

6 *concessive clauses* (indicating 'although . . .'), expressed by *quamquam* and an indicative form, or by *quamvīs* or *cum* with a subjunctive:

canis, **quamquam ferōciter restitit**, ā lupō superātus est.
Although the dog resisted fiercely, it was overcome by the wolf.

cum in rīpā flūminis habitāret, tamen nāvigāre nesciēbat.
Although he lived on the bank of a river, he still didn't know how to sail.

Further examples:

1 quamquam marītus tuus in carcere adhūc retinētur, nōlī dēspērāre!
2 quamvīs morbō afflīgerētur, senex ad forum ambulāre cōnātus est.
3 mīlitēs, quamquam itinere fessī erant, ad pugnandum sē īnstrūxērunt.

> Sentences containing concessive clauses introduced by *etsī* 'even if, even though' are expressed in the same ways as conditional sentences (described in **24**):
>
> **etsī mihi mīlle dēnāriōs obtulissēs**, ānulum numquam tibi vēndidissem.
> Even if you had offered me a thousand denarii, I would never have sold you the ring.
>
> **etsī magna turba puellae obstābat**, ad portum mox pervēnit.
> Even though a large crowd obstructed the girl, she soon reached the port.

7 *comparative clauses*, expressed by *sīcut* 'just as' or *ut* 'as' (often accompanied by *ita* 'so') and an indicative form, to make a comparison with an *actual* event, or by *quasi, tamquam* 'as if, as though' and a subjunctive form, to make a comparison with an *imaginary* event:

servī in agrīs labōrābant, **sīcut dominus iusserat**.
The slaves were working in the fields, just as the master had ordered.

ut fēlēs mūrem petit, ita gladiātor adversārium agitāvit.
As a cat chases a mouse, so did the gladiator pursue his opponent.

centuriō mē salūtāvit **quasi amīcissimus essem**.
The centurion greeted me as if I were his dearest friend.

Further examples:

1 ut pater mē docuit, ita ego tē docēbō.
2 puerī fūgērunt quasi umbram vīdissent.
3 ut avēs per caelum volant, ita nāvēs per undās ruēbant.
4 amīcus meus erat victor, sīcut spērāveram.

> For examples of comparison expressed by *tantus . . . quantus*, *tot . . . quot*, etc., see paragraph 1 above.

8   *clauses of fear and danger*, introduced by *nē** followed by a subjunctive form to express a fear that something MAY happen, IS happening, or HAS happened:

> avārus verēbātur **nē fūr aurum invenīret**.
> The miser was afraid lest a thief would find his gold.†
> *or*, in more natural English:
> The miser was afraid that a thief would find his gold.

> perīculum est **nē barbarī oppidum capiant**.
> There is a danger that the barbarians may capture the town.†

> puellae timent **nē amīca in morbum gravem inciderit**.
> The girls fear that their friend has fallen seriously ill.

*nē nōn** (sometimes *ut*) is used to express fear that something may NOT happen, is NOT happening, or has NOT happened:

> timēbāmus { **nē pater nōn superfuisset**.
> { **ut pater superfuisset**.
> We were afraid that our father had not survived.

Further examples:

1   perīculum erat nē nāvēs tempestāte dēlērentur.
2   mercātor timēbat nē iuvenis pecūniam nōn redderet.
3   timeō nē nūntius ab hostibus captus sit.
4   verēbāmur nē parentēs nostrī in flammīs periissent.

> For an example of another way of using verbs meaning 'I am afraid', see **21**.1.

---

* The reason why *nē* is used for a POSITIVE fear, and *nē nōn* (or *ut*) for a NEGATIVE fear, is that clauses of fear are used to express a wish, and the speaker wishes the *opposite* of what he fears. For example, 'I fear that he may find me' implies 'May he *not* find me!' and the Latin is *timeō nē mē inveniat*.

†These sentences could also mean '. . . was afraid that a thief *was* finding his gold' and '. . . danger that the barbarians *are* capturing the town'. The surrounding context normally makes the speaker's meaning clear.

9   Further examples of the types of subordinate clause described in
    paragraphs 1–8:

> 1 servī in viam contendērunt ut pompam spectārent.
> 2 sacerdōs, postquam victimam sacrificāvit, deōs precātus est.
> 3 quamquam ancilla suāviter cantābat, hospitēs nōn dēlectābantur.
> 4 tam obscūra est nox ut nihil vidēre possim.
> 5 medicus, cum dentēs meōs extrāxisset, duōs dēnāriōs postulāvit.
> 6 faber diū tacēbat, quasi rem difficillimam cōgitāret.
> 7 spectātōrēs āthlētam vituperābant quod fraude vīcerat.
> 8 spectātōrēs āthlētam vituperābant quod fraude vīcisset.
> 9 fugite, nē ab inimīcīs interficiāminī!
> 10 agricola, cum ad vīllam regrederētur, lupum ingentem cōnspexit.
> 11 homō cuius domus ardēbat auxilium ā praetereuntibus petīvit.
> 12 rēgīna, quamvīs īrāta esset, mihi tandem ignōvit.
> 13 fēmina magistrum ēlēgit quī fīliōs docēret.
> 14 timēbāmus nē ab hostibus circumvenīrēmur.
> 15 eī quī mentīrī solent, saepe ipsī dēcipiuntur.
> 16 iuvenēs frūstrā exspectābant dōnec amīcus redīret.

What type of subordinate clause is being used in each example?

10   For examples of subordinate clauses used to express indirect question
     and indirect command, see **25**.2 and 3.

11   For examples of subordinate clauses used inside indirect speech, see
     25.7.

12   For examples of conditional clauses, see **24**.1–2.

24 Conditional sentences

Normally made up of (i) a main clause, and (ii) a conditional cla
introduced by *sī* 'if' or *nisi* 'unless, if . . . not':

1   *with indicative forms of the verb*

1a   *in a past tense*
   sī amīcus tuus testāmentum **fīnxit**, scelus grave **commīsit**.
   If your friend forged the will, he has committed a serious crime.

1b   *in the present tense*
   sī **valēs, gaudeō**.
   If you are well, I am pleased.

1c   *in the future or future perfect tense* (often translated in a conditional
clause by an English present tense)
   sī illud iterum **fēceris**, tē **pūniam**.
   If you do that again, I shall punish you.

   sī in urbe **manēbit**, in perīculō **erit**.
   If he stays in the city, he will be in danger.

   nisi imperātor novās cōpiās **mīserit**, **opprimēmur**.
   If the emperor does not send reinforcements, we shall be
      overwhelmed.
   or, Unless the emperor sends reinforcements, we shall be
      overwhelmed.

Further examples:

1 sī ancilla dormit, excitā eam!
2 sī dē equō tuō dēcideris, cēterī puerī tē dērīdēbunt.
3 sī frātrēs meī in Britanniā mīlitābunt, miserrimī erunt.
4 nisi nāvēs ad portum mox pervēnerint, tempestāte dēlēbuntur.

1d   *in two different tenses* (main clause referring to one time, and conditional
   clause to another):
   sī aeger **es**, medicum **arcessam**.
   If you are ill, I will send for a doctor.

2 *with subjunctive forms of the verb* (normally translated in the main clause by an English form involving 'would' or 'should')

2a *in the pluperfect tense of the subjunctive,* referring to PAST time:
sī in eōdem locō **mānsissēs**, perīculum **vītāvissēs**.
If you had stayed in the same place, you would have avoided the danger.

sī dīligentius **labōrāvissem**, dominus mē **līberāvisset**.
If I had worked harder, my master would have freed me.

magister, nisi nimis vīnī **bibisset**, in flūmen nōn **cecidisset**.
If the teacher had not drunk too much wine, he would not have fallen into the river.

Further examples:

1 sī equōs vēndidissēs, multam pecūniam accēpissēs.
2 nisi coquus circumspectāvisset, cibus ā cane raptus esset.
3 sī nūntiī māne profectī essent, Londinium ante noctem pervēnissent.
4 sī Caesar nōbīs praefuisset, hostēs superāvissēmus.

2b *in the imperfect tense of the subjunctive,* referring to PRESENT time:
sī Rōmae nunc **habitārem**, clientēs mē assiduē **vexārent**.
If I were living in Rome now, my clients would be continually pestering me.

sī Domitiānus nōs adhūc **regeret**, miserrimī **essēmus**.
If Domitian were still ruling us, we should be very unhappy.

Further examples:

1 sī soror mea nunc vīveret, tē adiuvāret.
2 sī mīlitēs vōs in itinere comitārentur, minus sollicitus dē vōbīs essem.

2c *in the present tense of the subjunctive,* referring to FUTURE time:
sī hanc medicīnam **bibās**, statim **convalēscās**.
If you were to drink this medicine, you would get better at once.

sī piscēs per aera **volent**, omnēs **mīrentur**.
If fish were to fly through the air, everyone would be amazed.

Further examples:

1 sī imperātōrem occīdere cōnēris, ipse statim interficiāris.
2 pater meus, sī cognōscat quid fēcerim, mē sevērissimē pūniat.

2d *in two different tenses of the subjunctive (pluperfect and imperfect),* referring to a mixture of PAST and PRESENT time:
nisi mē **invēnissēs**, etiam nunc ibi **stārem**.
If you hadn't found me, I should still be standing there now.

25 Indirect speech

1 *summary of differences between direct and indirect speech*

	direct	indirect
question	'quid facis?'	rogāvī hominem quid faceret.
	'What are you doing?'	I asked the man what he was doing.
command	'pugnāte!'	dux iuvenibus imperāvit ut pugnārent.
	'Fight!'	The leader ordered the young men to fight.
statement	'poēta recitat.'	puer dīcit poētam recitāre.
	'A poet is reciting.'	The boy says that a poet is reciting.

2 *indirect questions*, expressed by a question-word such as *quis* 'who' or *num* 'whether',* followed by a subjunctive form of the verb:†

senex nesciēbat **quis templum aedificāvisset**.
The old man did not know who had built the temple.

    (Compare this with the direct question: 'quis templum aedificāvit?')

mē rogāvērunt **num satis pecūniae habērem**.
They asked me whether I had enough money.

    (Compare: 'satis pecūniae habēs?')

in animō volvēbam **quid māter dictūra esset**.
I was wondering what my mother would say, *or* was going to say.

    (Compare: 'quid māter dīcet?' and for further examples of this use of the future participle, see **7d**.4.)

necne is used in indirect questions to mean 'or not':
incertī erant **utrum dux vīveret necne**.
They were unsure whether their leader was alive or not.

    (Compare: 'utrum dux vīvit annōn?')

Further examples:
1 magister scīre vult quis fenestram frēgerit.
2 puella hominem rogāvit quot piscēs cēpisset.
3 incertī sumus quārē cīvēs ad templum prōgrediantur.
4 dux nesciēbat quid hostēs factūrī essent.
5 cognōscere cōnābar num fēmina marītum occīdisset.

---

* For examples of *num* used (with a different meaning) in *direct* questions, see **11**.6.

† A question-word and subjunctive can also be used with such verbs as *rogō, scio, nescio*, etc. to express *indirect deliberative questions*. (Direct deliberative questions are described in **11**.7.)
For example, *nesciēbam quid facerem* could mean either 'I didn't know what I was doing' (indirect question) or 'I didn't know what to do' (indirect deliberative question). Usually the context of the sentence makes it clear what the speaker means; if it doesn't, the speaker can make the meaning clear by using a different form of words (e.g. the gerundive, as described in **26**.2b, *nesciēbam quid faciendum esset* 'I didn't know what ought to be done').

3   *indirect commands,** usually expressed by *ut* or *nē* followed by a
subjunctive form in the present or imperfect tense:

> rēx mīlitibus imperāvit **ut captīvōs līberārent**.
> The king ordered the soldiers that they should set the prisoners free.
> *or*, in more natural English:
> The king ordered the soldiers to set the prisoners free.

> (Compare this with the direct command: 'captīvōs līberāte!')

> puella mercātōrem ōrāvit **ut pecūniam redderet**.
> The girl begged the merchant to give the money back.

> (Compare: 'pecūniam redde!')

> lēgātus barbarōs hortātus est **ut mōrēs Rōmānōs discerent**.
> The governor encouraged the barbarians to learn Roman ways.

> (Compare: 'mōrēs Rōmānōs discite!')

> ab amīcīs monēmur **nē haruspicibus crēdāmus**.
> We are advised by friends not to believe the soothsayers.

> (Compare: 'nōlīte haruspicibus crēdere!')

Indirect commands introduced by the verbs *iubeō* and *vetō* are
expressed not by *ut* or *nē* and the subjunctive but by the infinitive:

> domina servum iussit fenestram **reficere**.
> The mistress ordered the slave to mend the window.

> spectātōrēs vetābantur cibum bestiīs **dare**.
> The spectators were forbidden to feed the animals.
> *or*, The spectators were told not to feed the animals.

Further examples:

1 dominus ancillīs imperāvit ut vīnum ferrent.
2 agricola nōs monuit ut prīmā lūce proficīscerēmur.
3 sacerdōs puerōs vetuit in templō loquī.
4 amīcī mihi persuādēre cōnantur nē in hōc oppidō maneam.
5 senex nautam hortābātur ut nāvem vēnderet et tabernam emeret.

---

* Indirect commands can be introduced not only by verbs meaning 'I order',
'I demand', etc. but also by verbs meaning 'I beg', 'I persuade', 'I request',
'I warn', etc.

4 *indirect statements*, normally expressed by a noun or pronoun in the accusative case and an infinitive form of the verb:

4a *introduced by a verb in the present or future tense*	4b *introduced by a verb in a past tense*
with the present active infinitive	
crēdō prīncipem Agricolae **invidēre**.	crēdēbam prīncipem Agricolae **invidēre**.
I believe the emperor *to be jealous* of Agricola.	I believed the emperor *to be jealous* of Agricola.
or, in more natural English:	*or*, in more natural English:
I believe that the emperor *is jealous* of Agricola.	I believed that the emperor *was jealous* of Agricola.

(Compare these with the direct statement: 'prīnceps Agricolae invidet.')

with the present passive infinitive

scit multās prōvinciās ā latrōnibus **vexārī**.	sciēbat multās prōvinciās ā latrōnibus **vexārī**.
He knows that many provinces *are troubled* by bandits.	He knew that many provinces *were troubled* by bandits.

(Compare: 'multae prōvinciae ā latrōnibus vexantur.')

with the perfect active infinitive

centuriō hostēs dīcit **cōnstitisse**.	centuriō hostēs dīxit **cōnstitisse**.
The centurion says that the enemy *have halted*.	The centurion said that the enemy *had halted*.

(Compare: 'hostēs cōnstitērunt.')

with the perfect passive infinitive

vir uxōrem **servātam esse** putat.	vir uxōrem **servātam esse** putāvit.
The man thinks that his wife *has been saved*.	The man thought that his wife *had been saved*.

(Compare: 'uxor servāta est.')

with the future active infinitive

senātōrēs prō certō habent cīvēs numquam **cessūrōs esse**.	senātōrēs prō certō habēbant cīvēs numquam **cessūrōs esse**.
The senators are sure that the citizens *will* never *give in*.	The senators were sure that the citizens *would* never *give in*.

(Compare: 'cīvēs numquam cēdent.')

with the future infinitive passive

captīvōs **interfectum īrī** nūntiat.	captīvōs **interfectum īrī** nūntiābat.
He is announcing that the prisoners *will be killed*.	He was announcing that the prisoners *would be killed*.

(Compare: 'captīvī interficientur.')

4c   Indirect statements introduced by verbs meaning 'I hope', 'I promise', 'I threaten', etc. are normally expressed in Latin by an accusative and future infinitive (whereas English usually prefers a shorter form):

> spērō **mē ventūrum esse**.
> I hope that I shall come.
> *or*, in more natural English: I hope to come.

> pollicitī sunt **sē discessūrōs esse**.
> They promised that they would go away.
> *or*, in more natural English: They promised to go away.

4d   Forms of *sē*, *suus* and *is* are used in the following ways in indirect statements:

> Marcus dīcit **sē** in Britanniā habitāre.
> Marcus says that he (i.e. Marcus) lives in Britain.

> Marcus dīcit **eum** in Britanniā habitāre.
> Marcus says that he (i.e. someone else) lives in Britain.

> agricolae affirmāvērunt vīllās **suās** incēnsās esse.
> The farmers claimed that their (i.e. the farmers') villas had been burnt.

> agricolae affirmāvērunt vīllās **eōrum** incēnsās esse.
> The farmers claimed that their (i.e. other people's) villas had been burnt.

4e   *negō* 'I deny, I say that . . . not' is used in the following way:

> iuvenis negāvit sē pecūniam perdidisse.
> The young man denied that he had wasted the money.
> *or*, The young man said that he had not wasted the money.

Further examples:

1 servus dīcit ingentem nāvem portuī appropinquāre.
2 omnēs cīvēs crēdēbant Claudium venēnō necātum esse.
3 mercātor spērābat sē magnās dīvitiās in Hispāniā comparātūrum esse.
4 senātōrēs sciunt bellum terribile contrā Britannōs gerī.
5 audiō decem hominēs herī damnātōs esse.
6 amīcus meus putat urbem mox captum īrī.
7 homō clāmābat tabernam suam ardēre.
8 testis negāvit eum senī umquam nocuisse.
9 polliceor mē fenestram crās refectūrum esse.
10 fēmina suspicābātur puerum mentīrī.

5   For examples of different types of word order involving indirect speech and verbs meaning 'I ask', 'I order', 'I say', etc., see **28**.4.

6 Sometimes the verb which means 'I ask', 'I order', 'I say', etc. is omitted altogether, especially if one sentence in indirect speech is followed immediately by another. The use of the accusative and infinitive (or of the subjunctive) makes it clear that indirect speech is being used. For example:

> rēx dīxit Rōmānōs exercitum parāvisse; mox prīmōs mīlitēs adventūrōs esse.
> The king said that the Romans had prepared an army; (he said that) the first soldiers would soon arrive.

The verb *dīxit* is not repeated in the second part of the sentence, because the use of the accusative (*prīmōs mīlitēs*) and infinitive (*adventūrōs esse*) makes it clear that the sentence is still reporting what the king said.

> fēmina marītum monuit ut domō quam celerrimē discēderet; proficīscerētur ante prīmam lūcem; mīlitēs eum quaerere.
> The woman warned her husband to leave the house as quickly as possible; (she warned that) he should set out before dawn; (she said that) soldiers were looking for him.

The verb *monuit* is not repeated in the second part of the sentence, because the use of the subjunctive (*proficīscerētur*) makes it clear that the sentence is still reporting the woman's warning; and in the last part of the sentence the accusative (*mīlitēs*) and infinitive (*quaerere*) make it clear that this is a further report of what the woman said.

7 In indirect speech, the verb in a subordinate clause is normally subjunctive:

> mercātor respondit servōs quī vīnum **effunderent** magnō pretiō ēmptōs esse.
> The merchant replied that the slaves who were pouring out the wine had been bought at a high price.

> (Compare this with the direct statement: 'servī quī vīnum effundunt magnō pretiō ēmptī sunt.')

> spectātōrēs affirmant Milōnem victūrum esse, quod cotīdiē sē **exerceat**.
> The spectators claim that Milo will win, because he trains every day.

> (Compare: 'Milō vincet, quod cotīdiē sē exercet.')

26 Uses of the gerund, gerundive and supine

1 *gerund* (*portandum* 'carrying', *docendum* 'teaching', etc.), used in the following cases:

accusative with *ad* (meaning 'for the purpose of . . .')
multī hominēs ad **audiendum** aderant.
Many men were there for the purpose of listening.
or, in more natural English:
Many men were there to listen.

genitive
optimam habeō occāsiōnem **cognōscendī** quid acciderit.
I have an excellent opportunity of finding out what has happened.

dative
operam **scrībendō** dedit.
He gave his attention to writing.

ablative
prūdenter **emendō** et **vēndendō**, pater meus dīvitissimus factus est.
By buying and selling sensibly, my father became very rich.

Further examples:
1 trēs mīlitēs tabernam ad bibendum ingressī sunt.
2 omnēs hominēs dēbent artem bene dīcendī discere.
3 ancilla tua, fidēliter decem annōs serviendō, lībertātem meruit.
4 iūdex mihi nūllam occāsiōnem respondendī dedit.
5 puerī senem clāmandō vexāvērunt.

2 *gerundive* (*portandus, docendus,* etc.):

2a *meaning 'being carried', 'being taught', etc.,* used in the following cases:

accusative with *ad*
iuvenis ad epistulam **legendam** cōnsēdit.
The young man sat down for the purpose of the letter being read.
or, in more natural English:
The young man sat down to read the letter.

genitive
nāvis **servandae** causā, magnam mercis partem in mare ēiēcērunt.
For the sake of the ship being saved, they jettisoned a large part of
the cargo.
or, in more natural English:
To save the ship, they jettisoned a large part of the cargo.

dative
mīlitēs omnem operam armīs **parandīs** dabant.
The soldiers were giving all their attention to preparing their weapons.

ablative
custōdibus **dēcipiendīs**, ē carcere effūgī.
By deceiving the guards, I escaped from the prison.

Further examples:

1 frāter meus in rīpā flūminis sedēre solēbat, ad piscēs capiendōs.
2 Caesar artem bellī gerendī bene sciēbat.
3 fabrī omnem operam templō perficiendō dabant.
4 amīcīs servandīs, centuriō magnam glōriam adeptus est.
5 avārus occāsiōnem pecūniae recipiendae āmīsit.

2b *meaning 'needing to be carried', 'needing to be done', etc.*, often used in the nominative case with some form of the verb *sum* and known as the *gerundive of obligation*:

    discipulī **interrogandī** sunt.

        The pupils are needing to be questioned.
        or, in more natural English:
        The pupils must be questioned.

The dative is used to indicate the person who has to do the action:

    longum iter mihi **faciendum** erat.*   I had to make a long journey.
    vīlla nōbīs **aedificanda** est.*   We must build a villa.
    mīlitibus **cōnsistendum** erit.*   The soldiers will have to halt.

Further examples:

1 flammae exstinguendae sunt.
2 in hōc locō nōbīs pugnandum est.
3 nāvis tibi reficienda est.
4 servīs dīligenter labōrandum erat.
5 fundus mihi vēndendus erit.

3   *supine (portātum, doctum, etc.)* used in the following cases:

    accusative, used with verbs involving movement, indicating purpose:
        cīvēs **dormītum** abiērunt.
        The citizens went away to sleep.

    The accusative of the supine is also used with *īrī* (present passive infinitive of *eō* 'I go') to form the future passive infinitive:

        nūntius dīcit vīllam **dēlētum īrī**.
        The messenger says that there is a movement (*īrī*) to destroy the villa.
        or, in more natural English:
        The messenger says that the villa will be destroyed.

    ablative, used with certain adjectives:
        mōnstrum terribile **vīsū** erat.
        The monster was terrible to see.

---

* Sentences like these cannot be translated literally into natural English. For example, the literal translation of *longum iter mihi faciendum erat* would be something like 'There was a long journey for me, needing to be made', which sounds so peculiar that it must be rephrased as 'I had to make . . .' etc.

PART THREE

WORD ORDER AND SENTENCE STRUCTURE

27 Word order in short sentences

(examples of some common patterns and ways in which they can be varied)

1 *sentences consisting of a nominative noun and verb*

    1a *nominative + verb*
        custōdēs dormiēbant.   The guards were asleep.

    1b *verb + nominative*
        dēcidit rēx.   The king fell down.
                       or, Down fell the king.

2 *sentences consisting of two nouns (nominative and accusative) and a verb*

    2a *nominative + accusative + verb* (an extremely common word order)
        cīvēs templum vīsitābant.   The citizens were visiting the temple.

    2b *verb + accusative + nominative*
        dedit signum haruspex.   The soothsayer gave the signal.
                       or, It was the soothsayer who gave the signal.*

> A Roman could use this word order to emphasise *haruspex*. For example, he might guess that his readers (or listeners) would expect the signal to be given by the trumpeter, not by the soothsayer, and he might therefore choose to hold back the word *haruspex* so that the sentence ends with a surprise.

    2c *accusative + nominative + verb*
        equum agricola vēndidit.   The farmer sold the horse.
                       or, What the farmer sold was the horse.

> This word order could be used by a Roman who has just been asked 'What did the farmer sell?'; he might choose to start his reply with *equum* because it gives the answer to the question. Another reason for beginning with *equum* might be to emphasise a contrast with some other animal; for example, *equum . . . vēndidit* might be followed by *porcum retinuit*, 'The farmer sold the horse but kept the pig.'

---

* Other translations (of this and other sentences) are also possible, e.g. 'The person who gave the signal was the soothsayer.'

3 *sentences containing three nouns (nominative, accusative and dative) and a verb*

    3a *nominative + dative + accusative + verb* (a common order)
        mīles puerō gladium ostendit. The soldier showed his sword to the
                                       boy.

    3b *dative + nominative + accusative + verb*
        uxōrī mercātor nihil lēgāvit.   The merchant left nothing to his wife.
                                      or, To his wife the merchant left
                                          nothing.

> One of the reasons for which a writer might use this word order is to emphasise a contrast between *uxōrī* and another word. For example, *uxōrī . . . lēgāvit* might be followed by *lībertīs vīllam ingentem*, 'To his wife the merchant left nothing, but to his freedmen he left an enormous villa.'

    3c *accusative + verb + nominative + dative*
        grātiās ēgērunt cōnsulēs   The consuls thanked the slaves.
          servīs.   *or*, The people whom the consuls
                                        thanked were the slaves.

> In this sentence, *servīs* is placed last (a rather unusual position for a dative). There are various reasons why a writer might choose to do this. For example, instead of emphasising the fact that the consuls thanked anyone, he might want to emphasise that the ones who were thanked were (perhaps unexpectedly) the slaves.

4 Further examples of all the patterns in paragraphs 1–3:

    1 iuvenēs clāmōrem faciebant.   5 praemium dedit dominus coquō.
    2 intrāvit senex.   6 centuriōnēs proficīscēbantur.
    3 māter fīliō dōnum ēmit.   7 senātōribus spectātōrēs omnia
    4 ancillās iūdex laudāvit.   nārrāvērunt.
                                        8 interfēcit lupum Sextus.

5 *sentences which do not contain nominatives*

    5a *accusative + verb*
        candidātum salūtāvērunt.   They greeted the candidate.

    5b *dative + verb*
        amīcīs crēdidit.   He believed his friends.

    5c *dative + accusative + verb*
        nūntiō epistulam trādidī.   I handed a letter to the messenger.

Further examples:

    1 iānuam aperuērunt.   4 deae cōnfīdēbat.
    2 hospitibus vīnum offerēbam.   5 patrī dēnāriōs reddidī.
    3 nāvem reficiēbāmus.   6 captīvīs pepercērunt.

28 Word order in longer sentences

1 *relative clauses*

1a *following main clause*
prope āram stābant mīlitēs, **quī dūcem custōdiēbant**.
Near the altar stood the soldiers, who were guarding the leader.

1b *in middle of main clause*
uxor mea, **quae strepitum audīverat**, statim accurrit.
My wife, who had heard the din, came running up at once.

equum **quem āmīseram** repperī.
I found the horse which I had lost.

1c *in front of main clause* (normally with forms of *is* or *īdem* as the antecedent):
quī tē heri culpābat, is tē hodiē laudat.
The person who was blaming you yesterday is praising you today.

quae tibi coniūnx est, eadem mihi fīlia paene est.
The same woman who is a wife to you is virtually a daughter to
    me.

quae dominus iussit, ea servōs efficere oportet.
What the master has ordered, the slaves must carry out.
or, The slaves must carry out what the master has ordered.

Sometimes the antecedent is omitted altogether:
quod potuī, fēcī.   I have done what I could.
quī audet, vincit.   He who dares, wins.

Further examples:

1 ancillae, quibus domina magnum praemium prōmīserat, dīligenter labōrābant.
2 mercātor duōs coquōs ēmit, quōrum alter Graecus, alter Aegyptius erat.
3 quod rēx vōbīs heri dedit, id vōbīs crās auferet.
4 custōdēs quī dormīverant sevērissimē pūnīvī.
5 quī semper haesitat, nihil umquam efficit.

2 *other subordinate clauses, and phrases containing participles*

    2a *following main clause*

       spectātōrēs vehementer clāmāvērunt, **quod īrātissimī erant**.
       The spectators shouted loudly, because they were very angry.

       in mediō ātriō sedēbat pontifex maximus, **togam splendidam
          gerēns**.
       In the middle of the hall sat the chief priest, wearing a splendid
          toga.

    2b *in middle of main clause*

       medicus, **dum cēnat**, ad cubiculum prīncipis arcessītus est.
       While the doctor was dining, he was summoned to the emperor's
          bedroom.

    2c *in front of main clause*

       simulac rēx signum dedit, equitēs hastās coniēcērunt.
       As soon as the king gave the signal, the horsemen threw their
          spears.

Further examples:

1 Caesar praecōnī imperāvit ut nōmen victōris recitāret.
2 mīlitēs, undique circumventī, dē vītā dēspērābant.
3 quamquam nox erat obscūra, viaeque dēsertae, puella nōn timēbat.

3 *two or more subordinate clauses or phrases containing participles*

    3a *leading out of the main clause, and placed one after the other*

       dominus incertus erat **quō fūgisset servus**, *cūr abesset coquus*, QUOT
         DĒNARIĪ ABLĀTĪ ESSENT.
       The master was uncertain where the slave had fled to, why the
          cook was missing, and how many denarii had been stolen.

    3b *one leading out of the other, and placed after it*

       puerī timēbant, **quod prope iānuam iacēbat ingēns canis**,
         vehementer lātrāns.
       The boys were afraid because near the door was lying a huge dog,
          barking loudly.

    3c *one inside the other*

       ubi ā culīnā *in quā cēnāverat* **redībat**, centuriōnem cōnspexit.
       When he was returning from the kitchen in which he had been
          dining, he caught sight of the centurion.

Further examples:

1 fūr, cum ad cubiculum ubi senex dormīre solēbat pervēnisset, in
   līmine cōnstitit.
2 lēgātus mox cognōvit ubi hostēs castra posuissent, quot mīlitēs in
   castrīs essent, quis mīlitibus praeesset.
3 deōs precāta ut fīlium suum tūtum redūcerent, fēmina ē templō exiit.

4   *verbs meaning 'I ask', 'I order', 'I say', etc.*

4a *in front of indirect speech*
   ducem **ōrābant** nē vīllam incenderet. (*indirect command*)
   They were begging the leader not to set fire to the villa.

   haruspicēs **cognōscent** num ōmina bona sint. (*indirect question*)
   The soothsayers will find out whether the omens are good.

   nūntius respondit multa oppida dēlēta esse. (*indirect statement*)
   The messenger replied that many towns had been destroyed.

4b *in middle of indirect speech*
   multōs hospitēs **audiō** invītārī.
   I hear that many guests are being invited.

4c *following indirect speech*
   utrum custōs esset an carnifex, nēmō **sciēbat**.
   Whether he was a guard or an executioner, no one knew.

   iuvenem pecūniam redditūrum esse **cōnfīdimus**.
   We are sure that the young man will give the money back.

   māter puerōs nē silvam intrārent identidem **monuit**.
   The mother repeatedly warned the boys not to go into the wood.

Further examples:

1 cognōscere voluī quārē senex catēnīs vīnctus esset.
2 amīcum nostrum suspicābāmur nimis vīnī bibisse.
3 hospitēs senātōrī ut loquī dēsineret tandem persuāsērunt.
4 quot equitēs captī sint, incertum est.
5 medicus Claudium venēnō necātum esse crēdēbat.

29 Noun and adjective phrases

1 *noun and adjective*

   multus sanguis   much blood
   vir benignus   a kind man

   > Adjectives which indicate size or quantity (e.g. *magnus, multī*) are usually
   > placed before the noun they describe; other adjectives are usually placed
   > after. But the Romans did not observe this as a strict rule.

2 *noun and adjective separated by a preposition*

   mediīs in undīs   in the middle of the waves
   hanc ad tabernam   to this shop

3 *noun and adjective separated by one word or more* (this and the following patterns are particularly common in verse)

> nox erat, et caelō fulgēbat lūna serēnō. (*Horace*)
> It was night, and the moon was shining in a clear sky.

4 *two pairs of noun and adjective phrases, one following the other*

> atque *opere* in *mediō* **laetus** cantābat **arātor**.
> And the happy ploughman was singing in the middle of his work.

5 *two pairs of noun and adjective phrases, one inside the other*

> agna *lupōs* audit circum **stabula alta** *frementēs*. (*Ovid*)
> The lamb hears the wolves howling around the tall sheepfolds.

6 *two pairs of noun and adjective phrases, intertwined*

> cantātur *tōtā* **nōmen** in *urbe* **meum**.
> My name is sung all over the city.

The following type of intertwining is known as the 'golden line':

> 1st adjective + 2nd adjective + verb + 1st noun + 2nd noun

> **parvula** nē *nigrās* horrēscat **Erōtion** *umbrās*   (*Martial*)
> lest little Erotion should shudder at the dark shadows

7 Further examples of the patterns described in paragraphs 4–6:

1 *Midday in summer*
  in *mediō caelō* **Phoebus** iam **fervidus** ardet.

2 *The rapid building of Rome's city wall*
  et **novus** *exiguō tempore* **mūrus** erat. (*Ovid*)

3 *A courageous young sailor*
  nōn timet ingentēs iuvenis fortissimus undās.

4 *A workman is promised a hot bath*
  fessaque mox calidā membra lavābis aquā.

> calidus: hot   membrum: limb
> exiguus: small, short   Phoebus: Phoebus Apollo, i.e. the sun
> fervidus: intense, fierce

30 Omission of words from sentences

1 *omission of forms of* **sum** (e.g. *est, erat,* etc.)

    iam hōra diēī prīma.   Now it was the first hour of the day.

> (Compare this with a longer way of expressing the same idea:
> iam hōra diēī prīma erat.)

    multī occīsī, rēx captus.   Many were killed and the king was
                                captured.

> (Compare: multī occīsī sunt, rēx captus est.)

    sē dēceptum sēnsit.   He realised he had been deceived.

> (Compare: sē dēceptum esse sēnsit.)

2 *omission of forms of* **is** *as antecedents of* **quī**

    quod suscēpī, effēcī.   I have carried out what I undertook.

> (Compare: quod suscēpī, id effēcī, *or*, id quod suscēpī, effēcī.)
> For further examples, see **28**.1c.

3 *omission of word from one of two clauses*

3a *word omitted from second clause*
    Britannī cibum laudāvērunt, Rōmānī vīnum.
    The Britons praised the food, the Romans (praised) the wine.

> (Compare: Britannī cibum laudāvērunt, Rōmānī vīnum laudāvērunt.)

    plūrimī spectātōrēs gladiātōrem incitābant, nōnnūllī leōnem.
    Most spectators were encouraging the gladiator, some (were
       encouraging) the lion.

> (Compare: plūrimī spectātōrēs gladiātōrem incitābant, nōnnūllī leōnem
> incitābant.)

3b *word omitted from first clause*
    sacerdōs templum, poēta tabernam quaerēbat.
    The priest was looking for a temple, the poet (was looking) for an
       inn.

> (Compare: sacerdōs templum quaerēbat, poēta tabernam quaerēbat.)

    et movet ipse suās et nātī respicit ālās. (*Ovid*)
    He both moves his own wings himself and looks back at those of
       his son.

> (Compare: et ipse suās ālās movet et ālās nātī respicit.)

Further examples:
1 iuvenis taurum dūcēbat, puella equum.
2 sī dōnum imperātōris recūsābis, stultus eris; sī accipiēs, prūdēns.
3 aliī pecūniam, aliī glōriam petunt.
4 haec est statua illīus deae, quam Britannī Sūlem, Rōmānī Minervam
  vocant.

PART FOUR

MISCELLANEOUS

31 Notes on pronunciation

1   *short vowels*

    a   as in English* '*a*ha' or 'c*u*p'
    e   as in English 'p*e*t'
    i   as in English 'd*i*p'†
    o   as in English 'p*o*t'
    u   as in English 'p*u*t'
    y   as in French 'pl*u*me'§

Practice examples: agit, bonus, lyricus, medius, pater

2   *long vowels* (marked with a macron (ˉ) in this and other reference books)

    ā   as in English '*fa*ther'
    ē   as in French 'fianc*ée*'
    ī   as in English 'd*ee*p'
    ō   as in French '*beau*' (roughly as in English 'c*oa*t')
    ū   as in English 'f*oo*l' (NOT as in 'm*u*sic')

Practice examples: dē, fūr, māter, mīrābilis, tōtus

3   *diphthongs* (two vowels sounded together in a single syllable)

    ae   as in English 'h*i*gh'
    au   as in English 'h*ow*'
    ei   as in English 'd*ay*'
    eu   no exact English equivalent: 'e' is combined with 'oo', rather like 'ground' in some southern dialects (NOT as in 'f*ew*')
    oe   as in English 'b*oy*'
    ui   no exact English equivalent: 'u' is combined with 'i'

Practice examples: aeger, deinde, ēheu, foedus, huic, nauta

---

* In these notes, the word 'English' refers to the 'standard' pronunciation of southern British English (sometimes known as 'Received Pronunciation' or 'RP').

†If i is followed by a vowel (e.g. in *iam*), it is being used as a consonant and is pronounced in the way described in paragraph 4.

§y was used by the Romans in certain words taken over from Greek; long and short y had the same pronunciation.

4 *consonants*

   b   (usually) as in English '*b*ig'

   b   (followed by t or s) as in English 'li*p*s'

   c   as in English '*c*at' or '*k*ing' (NOT as in '*c*entre' or '*c*ello')

   ch as in English '*c*at' pronounced with emphasis ("You *c*at!") (NOT
         as in '*ch*in')

   g   as in English '*g*ot' (NOT as in '*g*entle')

   gn as 'ngn' in English 'ha*ngn*ail'

   i   (sometimes written as j) as in English '*y*ou'

   n   (usually) as in English '*n*et'

   n   (before c, g or qu) as in English 'a*n*ger'

   ph as in English '*p*ig' pronounced with emphasis ("*P*ig!") (NOT as
         in '*ph*oto')

   qu as in English '*qu*ick'

   r   as in Scottish ('rolled') pronunciation of 'bi*r*d'

   s   as in English '*s*ing' (NOT as in 'ro*s*es')

   th as in English '*t*errible' pronounced with emphasis ("*T*errible!")
         (NOT as in '*th*e' or '*th*eatre')

   v   (often written as u) as in English '*w*ind'

   x   as in English 'bo*x*'

Other consonants are pronounced as in English.

Practice examples: caelum, chorus, cīvēs, Ephesus, fabrī, iānua, ingēns, magnus, nūntius, obtineō, quī, regiō, rēx, theātrō, urbs, via

5 *doubled consonants*

Both consonants are pronounced. For example:

   ll as in English 'hall-light' (NOT as in 'taller')

   nn as in English 'thin-nosed' (NOT as in 'dinner')

   pp as in English 'hip-pocket' (NOT as in 'happy')

Practice examples: aggredior, annus, occupō, pessimus, supplicium, vīlla

6 *word stress* (indicated in this paragraph by an accent (´))

6a In a word of two syllables, the stress falls on the first syllable, e.g. ámō, ámās, etc.

6b In a word of three or more syllables, the stress falls on the second syllable from the end if that syllable is *heavy* (i.e. contains (i) a long vowel, OR (ii) a diphthong, OR (iii) a short vowel followed by two consonants or x or z), e.g. portámus, cōnféctus.

6c In all other words of three or more syllables, the stress falls on the third syllable from the end, e.g. amīcítia, cōnspíciō.

Practice examples: amīcus, ancilla, equus, fīlius, leō, mercātor, monēbant, monent, rēgīna, sacerdōs, trahet

32 How to use a Latin–English dictionary*

1   *nouns* (and some pronouns) are normally listed in the following way:
nominative singular : genitive singular : gender† : meaning

So, if the following information is given:
pāx, pācis, f. – peace
pāx means 'peace', *pācis* means 'of peace' and the word is feminine.

The genitive singular always shows the declension to which a noun belongs, and so can be used (together with a table of nouns if necessary, such as the ones in **1.**1–5) to identify the case or cases indicated by a particular ending.

Example 1a : dominus
dictionary entry : dominus, dominī, m. – master
This shows that *dominus* is a second-declension noun (like *servus*, shown in **1.**2) and so *dominus* must be nominative singular.

Example 1b : corpus
dictionary entry : corpus, corporis, n. – body
This shows that *corpus* is a third-declension noun (like *tempus*, **1.**3) and so *corpus* is either nominative or vocative or accusative singular.

Example 1c : aedificium
dictionary entry : aedificium, aedificiī, n. – building
This shows that *aedificium* is a second-declension noun (like *templum*, **1.**2) and so *aedificium* is either nominative or vocative or accusative singular.

Example 1d : montium
dictionary entry : mōns, montis, m. – mountain
This shows that *mōns* is a third-declension noun (like *urbs*, **1.**3) and so *montium* must be genitive plural, meaning 'of the mountains'.

Example 1e : piscī
dictionary entry : piscis, piscis, m. – fish
This shows that *piscis* is a third-declension noun (like *cīvis*, **1.**3) and so *piscī* must be dative singular, meaning 'to a fish'.

Example 1f : amīcī
dictionary entry : amīcus, amīcī, m. – friend
This shows that *amīcus* is a second-declension noun (like *servus*, **1.**2) and so *amīcī* is either genitive singular ('of a friend') or nominative or vocative plural.

---

* All Latin–English dictionaries follow the general plan described in this section, though they sometimes differ from each other slightly in small details of layout, etc.

† The abbreviation 'pl.' after the gender indicates that the noun is normally used only in its plural forms. For example: castra, castrōrum, n.pl. – camp

Exercise Use a dictionary (and, if necessary, the tables in **1**.1–5) to identify the cases of the following:

1 auctōrī	3 populō	5 capitis
2 hortī	4 virgō	6 silvīs

2 *adjectives of the first and second declension* (and most pronouns) are normally listed in the following way:

nominative masculine singular : nominative feminine singular : nominative neuter singular : meaning

So, if the following information is given:
   superbus, superba, superbum – proud
superbus is the masculine form, *superba* the feminine, and *superbum* the neuter, of the nominative singular.

3 *adjectives of the third declension* are normally listed in one of the following ways:

(i) nominative masculine singular : nominative feminine singular : nominative neuter singular : meaning

So, if the following information is given:
   ācer, ācris, ācre – sharp, keen
ācer is the masculine, *ācris* the feminine, and *ācre* the neuter form, of the nominative singular.

(ii) nominative masculine and feminine singular : nominative neuter singular : meaning

So, if the following information is given:
   fortis, forte – brave
fortis is the masculine and feminine, and *forte* the neuter form, of the nominative singular.

(iii) nominative singular (all genders) : genitive singular (all genders) : meaning

So, if the following information is given:
   ferōx, ferōcis – fierce (sometimes with '*gen.*' before the genitive)
ferōx is the nominative singular, and *ferōcis* the genitive singular, of all three genders.

4   *verbs* are usually listed in the following way:

the 1st person singular of the present tense;
the infinitive;
the 1st person singular of the perfect tense;
the supine;
the meaning.

So, if the following information is given:
   pōnō, pōnere, posuī, positum – place
pōnō means 'I place', *pōnere* means 'to place', *posuī* means 'I placed' and *positum* is the supine (whose use is described in **26**.3).

These four forms are known as the *principal parts* of a verb. All the forms of a normal verb can be identified if its principal parts are known (supplemented if necessary by reference to tables of verbs, such as those in **7 – 9**). The supine is not often met, but is used in forming some very important parts of the verb, such as the perfect passive participle. For example, *positus* ('having been placed') is formed from the supine *positum*.*

Example 4a : neglexistī
dictionary entry : neglegō, neglegere, neglexī, neglēctum – neglect
This shows that *neglexistī* is from the perfect tense of *neglegō* and so means 'you (singular) neglected'.

Example 4b : monitus erat
dictionary entry : moneō, monēre, monuī, monitum – advise, warn
This shows that *monitus erat* is from the pluperfect passive of *moneō* and so means 'he had been advised, warned'.

The principal parts, listed in the dictionary, can be used to check which conjugation a verb belongs to, and thus translate its tense correctly.

Example 4c : iubet
dictionary entry : iubeō, iubēre, iussī, iussum – order
This shows that *iubeō* is a *second*-conjugation verb (like *doceō*, shown in **7**) and so *iubet* must be a *present* tense and means 'he orders'.

Example 4d : dūcet
dictionary entry : dūcō, dūcere, dūxī, ductum – lead
This shows that *dūcō* is a *third*-conjugation verb (like *trahō* in **7**) and so *dūcet* must be a *future* tense and means 'he will lead'.

Exercise Use a dictionary (and, if necessary, the tables in **7**) to identify the tenses of the following, then translate them:

1 exercet	3 cōgētis	5 prohibēmur
2 scindet	4 persuādētis	6 mittēmur

---

* If a verb has no supine and no perfect passive participle, only the first three principal parts are usually listed.

5 *deponent verbs* are listed in the following way:

the 1st person singular of the present tense;
the infinitive;
the 1st person singular of the perfect tense;
the meaning.

So, if the following information is given:
    sequor, sequī, secūtus sum – follow
sequor means 'I follow', *sequī* means 'to follow' and *secūtus sum* means 'I followed'.

The principal parts, listed in the dictionary, can be used to check whether a word with a passive ending (e.g. *ēgrediuntur, custōdiuntur*) comes from a deponent verb or not.

Example 5a : ēgrediuntur
dictionary entry : ēgredior, ēgredī, ēgressus sum – go out
It is clear from the listed forms that *ēgredior* is a *deponent* verb; *ēgrediuntur* must therefore have an *active* meaning, i.e. 'they go out'.

Example 5b : custōdiuntur
dictionary entry : custōdiō, custōdīre, custōdīvī, custōdītum – guard
It is clear from the listed forms that *custōdiō* is *not* a deponent verb; *custōdiuntur* must therefore have a *passive* meaning, i.e. 'they are being guarded'.

Exercise Translate the following, using a dictionary to check whether they are deponent verbs or not, and referring if necessary to the tables in **7** and **8**:

1 sequitur	3 vocābar	5 ingressī sunt
2 relinquitur	4 mīrābar	6 oppressī sunt

6 Verbs used with a direct object (see **14**.3a), e.g. *laudō*, are known as *transitive* verbs, indicated in many dictionaries by *tr.*; verbs used without a direct object, e.g. *currō*, are known as *intransitive* verbs, indicated by *intr.*

7 Adjectives and verbs used with the genitive, dative or ablative cases are indicated by +*gen.*, +*dat.* and +*abl.* respectively.

8 Prepositions used with the accusative case, such as *trāns*, are indicated by +*acc.*; those used with the ablative, such as *ex*, are indicated by +*abl.*

9 Some Latin words can be spelt in more than one way. In particular, verbs beginning with such prefixes as ab-, ad-, con-, in- or sub-, followed by a consonant, sometimes change the last letter of the prefix for ease of pronunciation (e.g. *inpellō* can become *impellō*, *abferō* always becomes *auferō*, *adtollō* is usually spelt *attollō* and *conlocō collocō*), or drop the last letter of the prefix altogether (e.g. *adspiciō* is usually spelt *aspiciō*).

So (for example),
words not listed with the spelling *adc* . . .   may be listed under *acc* . . .

"	"	"	*adf* . . .	"	"	*aff* . . .
"	"	"	*adg* . . .	"	"	*agg* . . .
"	"	"	*adl* . . .	"	"	*all* . . .
"	"	"	*adp* . . .	"	"	*app* . . .
"	"	"	*adsc* . . .	"	"	*asc* . . .
"	"	"	*adsp* . . .	"	"	*asp* . . .
"	"	"	*conl* . . .	"	"	*coll* . . .
"	"	"	*conm* . . .	"	"	*comm* . . .
"	"	"	*inl* . . .	"	"	*ill* . . .
"	"	"	*inm* . . .	"	"	*imm* . . .
"	"	"	*inp* . . .	"	"	*imp* . . .
"	"	"	*inr* . . .	"	"	*irr* . . .
"	"	"	*subm* . . .	"	"	*summ* . . .

and vice versa.

33 Summary of subjunctive uses*

1 *in main clauses*

1a *deliberative questions* (described in **11.**7):

quid **dīcam**? What am I to say?
utrum **pugnēmus** an **fugiāmus**? Should we fight or run away?
equitem an **ambulem**? Should I go on horseback or walk?

1b *jussive subjunctive* (**12.**3):

lūdōs **spectēmus**! Let us watch the games!
epistulam statim **recitet**. Let him read out the letter at once.
or, He is to read out the letter at once.

1c *wishes* (**13**):

utinam **mānsissēs**! If only you had stayed!
utinam nē **capiātur**! May he not get caught!

1d *in the main clause of some types of conditional sentence* (**24.**2):
mercātor, sī circumspectāvisset, fūrem **vīdisset**.
If the merchant had looked round, he would have seen the thief.

A subjunctive form of the verb is also used in the main clause of
sentences which *imply* a conditional clause without actually *stating* it:

tū ipse eīs **crēderēs**. You yourself would believe (*or* would have
believed) them (implying a conditional clause,
e.g. 'if you had been there', 'if you had heard
them', etc.)
aliquis hoc **dīcat** *or* Someone may say this . . . (implying, e.g., 'if he
dīxerit . . . wants to', 'if he disagrees with me', etc.)

This is sometimes described as the *potential* use of the subjunctive. The
pluperfect tense is used to refer to past time; the imperfect tense can refer
to either present or past time; the present and (sometimes) perfect tenses
are used to refer to future time.

Continued

* For further examples of each use, see the paragraph referred to under each
sub-heading.

Further examples:

1 loquar an taceam?
2 ad forum festīnēmus!
3 utinam iuvenis patrī pāruisset!
4 quō modō hostibus resistāmus?
5 sī servī aquam celeriter attulissent, domus flammīs nōn dēlēta esset.

2   *in subordinate clauses*

2a   *purpose clauses* (**23**.2):
hīc manēbō, ut vīllam **dēfendam**.
I shall stay here to defend the villa.

prīnceps Plīnium ēmīsit quī Bīthȳnōs **regeret**.
The Emperor sent Pliny out to rule the Bithynians.

tacēbāmus, nē ā centuriōne **audīrēmur**.
We kept quiet, in order not to be heard by the centurion.

2b   *result clauses* (**23**.3):
barbarī tot hastās coniēcērunt ut plūrimī equitēs **vulnerārentur**.
The barbarians threw so many spears that most horsemen were
    wounded.

2c   *causal clauses* with *cum* 'since', or with *quod* or *quia* to quote a reason
put forward by some other person or people (**23**.4):
cum clientēs meī **sītis**, subveniam vōbīs.
Since you are my clients, I will help you.

agricola fīlium castīgāvit quod plaustrum reficere nōn **cōnātus
    esset**.
The farmer scolded his son for not trying to mend the cart.

2d   *temporal clauses* with *cum* 'when', and with *priusquam, antequam,
dōnec* and *dum* to indicate purpose as well as time (**23**.5):
cum prōvinciam **circumīrem**, incendium Nīcomēdīae coortum est.
When I was going round the province, a fire broke out at
    Nicomedia.

abībō, priusquam ā dominō **agnōscar**.
I shall go away, before I am recognised by my master.

2e   *concessive clauses* with *quamvīs* or *cum* 'although' (**23**.6):
quamvīs multōs librōs **lēgerit**, nihil didicit.
Although he has read many books, he has learnt nothing.

2f   *comparative clauses*, making a comparison with an imaginary event
or situation (**23**.7):
per forum cucurrit quasi ā leōne **agitārētur**.
He ran through the forum as if he were being chased by a lion.

2g *clauses of fear or danger* (**23**.8):
verēbāmur nē omnēs nāvēs **dēlētae essent**.
We were afraid lest all the ships had been destroyed.
or, in more natural English:
We were afraid that all the ships had been destroyed.

perīculum est nē **occīdāris**.
There is a risk that you may be killed.

2h *conditional clauses* in conditional sentences whose translation
includes 'would' or 'should' (**24**.2):
sī dīves **essem**, nōn hīc habitārem.
If I were rich, I shouldn't be living here.

frāter meus, sī **certāvisset**, cēterōs facile vīcisset.
If my brother had competed, he would easily have beaten the
others.

2j *indirect questions* (**25**.2):
centuriō cognōscere vult ubi barbarī **cōnstiterint**.
The centurion wants to find out where the barbarians have halted.

2k *indirect commands* (**25**.3):
tē moneō ut lēgibus **pāreās**.
I advise you to obey the laws.

medicus nōbīs imperāvit nē **ingrederēmur**.
The doctor told us not to go in.

2m *subordinate clauses inside indirect speech* (**25**.7):
testis affirmāvit latrōnēs, postquam mercātōrem vehementer
    pulsāvissent, pecūniam rapuisse.
The witness declared that the robbers, after they had thumped the
    merchant violently, had seized his money.

Further examples:
1 tam saevus erat leō ut nēmō eī appropinquāre audēret.
2 cum dux mīlitēs īnstrūxisset, tuba sonuit.
3 custōdēs mē rogāvērunt quārē cōnsulem vīsitāre vellem.
4 māter puerīs imperāvit nē verba obscēna in mūrō scrīberent.
5 ad aulam contendimus ut veniam ā rēge peterēmus.
6 claudite portās castrōrum, priusquam hostēs intrent!
7 fabrī meī, quamvīs fessī sint, labōrāre nōn dēsinunt.
8 puella dīxit haruspicēs, postquam victimam īnspexissent, ōmina
  pessima nūntiāvisse.
9 servī laudābantur quia dominum ē perīculō servāvissent.
10 agricola attonitus cōnstitit, quasi porcum volantem cōnspicātus esset.
11 mercātor nāvem condūxit, quae frūmentum Rōmam veheret.
12 amīcī iuvenī persuāsērunt ut imperātōrem necāre cōnārētur.
13 sī pompam spectāvissētis, omnēs dēlectātī essētis.
14 valdē timēbam nē frāter meus ā iūdice damnārētur.
In each sentence, find the reason why a subjunctive is being used.

3   The tense of a subjunctive verb in a Latin subordinate clause depends on:

(i) the meaning, and

(ii) the tense of the verb in the main clause of the sentence, in accordance with the following rule, known as the rule of *sequence of tenses*:

If the verb in the main clause of the sentence is in a *primary* tense, i.e. present, future, perfect (meaning 'have . . .', e.g. *portāvī* 'I have carried') or future perfect, the tense of the subjunctive must normally be *present* or *perfect* (or, in indirect questions, present subjunctive of *sum* with a future participle);

If the verb in the main clause is in a *historic* (sometimes known as *secondary*) tense, i.e. imperfect, perfect (meaning '. . .ed', e.g. *portāvī* 'I carried') or pluperfect, the tense of the subjunctive must normally be *imperfect* or *pluperfect* (or, in indirect questions, imperfect subjunctive of *sum* with a future participle).

The following table summarises the various possible combinations of tense:

PRIMARY	*rogō*	I ask		*eum quid*	*scrībat*	he is writing
	rogābō	I shall ask		*him what*	*scrīpserit*	he has written
	rogāvī	I have asked			*scriptūrus*	he will write
	rogāverō	I shall have asked			*sit*	
HISTORIC	*rogābam*	I was asking		*eum quid*	*scrīberet*	he was writing
	rogāvī	I asked		*him what*	*scrīpsisset*	he had written
	rogāveram	I had asked			*scrīptūrus esset*	he would write

34 Principal parts* of some common verbs

Including examples (indented) of verbs extended by prefixes to form compound† verbs. Verbs which have similar ways of forming their 3rd or 4th principal parts are grouped together within each conjugation; so are deponent verbs:

1   *first conjugation*

    1a portō, portāre, portāvī, portātum – carry

    Many other first-conjugation verbs form their principal parts in the same way as *portō*. For example:

    amō, amāre, amāvī, amātum – love
    labōrō, labōrāre, labōrāvī, labōrātum – work
    pugnō, pugnāre, pugnāvī, pugnātum – fight
    rogō, rogāre, rogāvī, rogātum – ask

    1b secō, secāre, secuī, sectum – cut
        vetō, vetāre, vetuī, vetitum – forbid

    1c iuvō, iuvāre, iūvī, iūtum – help
        lavō, lavāre, lāvī, lautum (*sometimes* lavātum) – wash

    1d dō, dare, dedī, datum – give§
        stō, stāre, stetī, statum – stand
          adstō, adstāre, adstitī – stand by
          similarly: circumstō (stand around); obstō (stand in the way), etc.

    1e *deponent verbs*
        cōnor, cōnārī, cōnātus sum – try
        hortor, hortārī, hortātus sum – encourage
        minor, minārī, minātus sum – threaten
        moror, morārī, morātus sum – delay
        precor, precārī, precātus sum – pray (to)

2   *second conjugation*

    2a moneō, monēre, monuī, monitum – advise, warn

    Many other second-conjugation verbs form their principal parts in the same way as *moneō*. For example:

    dēbeō, dēbēre, dēbuī, dēbitum – owe, ought
    exerceō, exercēre, exercuī, exercitum – practise, exercise
    habeō, habēre, habuī, habitum – have
        prohibeō, prohibēre, prohibuī, prohibitum – prevent
    terreō, terrēre, terruī, territum – frighten

Continued

---

* For explanations of the term 'principal parts', see **32.4** and **32.5**.
†For an explanation of the spelling of some of these forms, see **32.9**.
§For examples of compounds of *dō*, see **34.3p**.

2b doceō, docēre, docuī, doctum – teach
teneō, tenēre, tenuī, tentum – hold
　　retineō, retinēre, retinuī, retentum – hold back

2c compleō, complēre, complēvī, complētum – fill
dēleō, dēlēre, dēlēvī, dēlētum – destroy
fleō, flēre, flēvī, flētum – weep

2d augeō, augēre, auxī, auctum – increase
fulgeō, fulgēre, fulsī – shine

2e ardeō, ardēre, arsī – be on fire
haereō, haerēre, haesī, haesum – stick, cling
iubeō, iubēre, iussī, iussum – order
maneō, manēre, mānsī, mānsum – remain
rīdeō, rīdēre, rīsī, rīsum – laugh, smile
suādeō, suādēre, suāsī, suāsum – advise
　　persuādeō, persuādēre, persuāsī, persuāsum – persuade

2f caveō, cavēre, cāvī, cautum – beware
faveō, favēre, fāvī, fautum – favour, support
moveō, movēre, mōvī, mōtum – move

2g respondeō, respondēre, respondī, respōnsum – reply

2h sedeō, sedēre, sēdī, sessum – sit
　　obsideō, obsidēre, obsēdī, obsessum – besiege
videō, vidēre, vīdī, vīsum – see
　　invideō, invidēre, invīdī, invīsum – envy

2j *deponent verbs*
polliceor, pollicērī, pollicitus sum – promise
vereor, verērī, veritus sum – be afraid
videor, vidērī, vīsus sum – seem

2k *semi-deponent verbs*
audeō, audēre, ausus sum – dare
gaudeō, gaudēre, gāvīsus sum – rejoice
soleō, solēre, solitus sum – be accustomed

2m Many of the verbs used impersonally which are listed in **19**.1 belong
to the second conjugation, with a 3rd person singular present
indicative ending in -*et* and a perfect ending in -*uit*. For example:

pudet mē　　　it makes me ashamed, I am ashamed
puduit mē　　　it made me ashamed, I was ashamed

3   *third conjugation*

3a trahō, trahere, trāxī, tractum – drag

Many other third-conjugation verbs form their principal parts in the
same way as *trahō*. For example:

dīcō, dīcere, dīxī, dictum – say
dūcō, dūcere, dūxī, ductum – lead
  circumdūcō, circumdūcere, circumdūxī, circumductum – lead around
  prōdūcō, prōdūcere, prōdūxī, prōductum – lead forward
  similarly: abdūcō (lead away); ēdūcō (lead out); indūcō (lead in); redūcō
      (lead back), etc.
intellegō, intellegere, intellēxī, intellēctum – understand
iungō, iungere, iūnxī, iūnctum – join
regō, regere, rēxī, rēctum – rule
  surgō, surgere, surrēxī, surrēctum – rise, get up

3b gerō, gerere, gessī, gestum – wear, carry
nūbō, nūbere, nūpsī, nūptum – marry
scrībō, scrībere, scrīpsī, scrīptum – write
sūmō, sūmere, sūmpsī, sūmptum – take
  cōnsūmō, cōnsūmere, cōnsūmpsī, cōnsūmptum – eat

3c cēdō, cēdere, cessī, cessum – give way
  discēdō, discēdere, discessī, discessum – depart
  prōcēdō, prōcēdere, prōcessī, prōcessum – advance
  similarly: accēdō (approach); incēdō (march); recēdō (withdraw), etc.
claudō, claudere, clausī, clausum – close
laedō, laedere, laesī, laesum – hurt, harm
lūdō, lūdere, lūsī, lūsum – play
mittō, mittere, mīsī, missum – send
  dīmittō, dīmittere, dīmīsī, dīmissum – send away, dismiss
  ēmittō, ēmittere, ēmīsī, ēmissum – send out
  similarly: āmittō (lose); dēmittō (send down); immittō (send in);
      remittō (send back); trānsmittō (send across), etc.
plaudō, plaudere, plausī, plausum – applaud
premō, premere, pressī, pressum – press
  opprimō, opprimere, oppressī, oppressum – crush
spargō, spargere, sparsī, sparsum – scatter

3d bibō, bibere, bibī – drink
comprehendō, comprehendere, comprehendī, comprehēnsum –
    grasp, seize
dēfendō, dēfendere, dēfendī, dēfēnsum – defend
incendō, incendere, incendī, incēnsum – burn
scandō, scandere – climb
  ascendō, ascendere, ascendī, ascēnsum – go up
  dēscendō, dēscendere, dēscendī, dēscēnsum – go down
scindō, scindere, scidī, scissum – tear
vertō, vertere, vertī, versum – turn
  animadvertō, animadvertere, animadvertī, animadversum – notice,
    turn attention to

3e arcessō, arcessere, arcessīvī*, arcessītum – summon, send for
    petō, petere, petīvī*, petītum – seek, make for, ask for
    quaerō, quaerere, quaesīvī*, quaesītum – look for, seek

3f colō, colere, coluī, cultum – cultivate, worship
    dēserō, dēserere, dēseruī, dēsertum – desert
    pōnō, pōnere, posuī, positum – put
      compōnō, compōnere, composuī, compositum – put together
      prōpōnō, prōpōnere, prōposuī, prōpositum – put forward
      similarly: circumpōnō (put round); dēpōnō (put down);
              expōnō (put out, explain); impōnō (put into, put onto);
              repōnō (put back), etc.
    recumbō, recumbere, recubuī – lie down

3g crēscō, crēscere, crēvī, crētum – grow
    nōscō, nōscere, nōvī, nōtum – get to know
      agnōscō, agnōscere, agnōvī, agnitum – recognise
      cognōscō, cognōscere, cognōvī, cognitum – find out, get to know
      ignōscō, ignōscere, ignōvī, ignōtum – forgive
    sinō, sinere, sīvī, sītum – allow
      dēsinō, dēsinere, dēsiī, dēsītum – stop, cease
    spernō, spernere, sprēvī, sprētum – despise, reject

3h agō, agere, ēgī, āctum – do, drive
      cōgō, cōgere, coēgī, coāctum – force, compel
    emō, emere, ēmī, ēmptum – buy
    frangō, frangere, frēgī, frāctum – break
    fundō, fundere, fūdī, fūsum – pour
      effundō, effundere, effūdī, effūsum – pour out
    legō, legere, lēgī, lēctum – read
      colligō, colligere, collēgī, collēctum – gather
      ēligō, ēligere, ēlēgī, ēlēctum – choose
    relinquō, relinquere, relīquī, relictum – leave
    rumpō, rumpere, rūpī, ruptum – break
      corrumpō, corrumpere, corrūpī, corruptum – spoil, corrupt
    vincō, vincere, vīcī, victum – conquer

3j sistō, sistere, stitī – bring to a halt, make to halt
      cōnsistō, cōnsistere, cōnstitī – stand still
      dēsistō, dēsistere, dēstitī – stop, cease
      resistō, resistere, restitī – resist

3k metuō, metuere, metuī – fear
    ruō, ruere, ruī – rush
    solvō, solvere, solvī, solūtum – untie
    statuō, statuere, statuī, statūtum – set up
      cōnstituō, cōnstituere, cōnstituī, cōnstitūtum – decide
      restituō, restituere, restituī, restitūtum – restore
    volvō, volvere, volvī, volūtum – roll

---

* sometimes shortened to *arcessiī*, *petiī* and *quaesiī*.

3m cadō, cadere, cecidī, cāsum – fall, die
    accidō, accidere, accidī – happen
    dēcidō, dēcidere, dēcidī – fall down
  caedō, caedere, cecīdī, caesum – cut, kill
    occīdō, occīdere, occīdī, occīsum – kill
  canō, canere, cecinī – sing
  currō, currere, cucurrī, cursum – run
    dēcurrō, dēcurrere, dēcurrī, dēcursum – run down
    recurrō, recurrere, recurrī, recursum – run back
    similarly: excurrō (run out); incurrō (run in); prōcurrō (run forward),
        etc.
  discō, discere, didicī – learn
  fallō, fallere, fefellī, falsum – deceive
  parcō, parcere, pepercī – spare, be merciful
  pellō, pellere, pepulī, pulsum – drive
    expellō, expellere, expulī, expulsum – drive out
    similarly: prōpellō (drive forward); repellō (drive back), etc.
  poscō, poscere, poposcī – demand
  tangō, tangere, tetigī, tāctum – touch
  tendō, tendere, tetendī, tentum – stretch
    contendō, contendere, contendī, contentum – hurry
    ostendō, ostendere, ostendī, ostentum – show

3p* reddō, reddere, reddidī, redditum – give back
    trādō, trādere, trādidī, trāditum – hand over
    similarly: addō (add); crēdō (believe); ēdō (give out); perdō (destroy,
        lose, waste); prōdō (betray); vēndō (sell); etc.

3q *deponent verbs*
  adipīscor, adipīscī, adeptus sum – obtain
  lābor, lābī, lāpsus sum – slip
  loquor, loquī, locūtus sum – speak
  nāscor, nāscī, nātus sum – be born
  oblīvīscor, oblīvīscī, oblītus sum – forget
  proficīscor, proficīscī, profectus sum – set out
  queror, querī, questus sum – complain
  sequor, sequī, secūtus sum – follow
  ūtor, ūtī, ūsus sum – use

3r *semi-deponent verbs*
  fīdō, fīdere, fīsus sum – trust
    cōnfīdō, cōnfīdere, cōnfīsus sum – have confidence in, trust
    diffīdō, diffīdere, diffīsus sum – distrust

---

* The verbs in **34**.3p are all compounds of *dō* (which was shown in **34**.1d).
dō is a *first*-conjugation verb (infinitive *dare*), but nearly all its compounds
belong to the *third* conjugation (infinitives *reddere, trādere,* etc.).

4   *fourth conjugation*

4a   audiō, audīre, audīvī*, audītum – hear

Many other fourth-conjugation verbs form their principal parts in the same way as *audiō*. For example:

custōdiō, custōdīre, custōdīvī*, custōdītum – guard
dormiō, dormīre, dormīvī*, dormītum – sleep
impediō, impedīre, impedīvī*, impedītum – hinder
pūniō, pūnīre, pūnīvī*, pūnītum – punish

4b   reperiō, reperīre, repperī, repertum – find
veniō, venīre, vēnī, ventum – come
    adveniō, advenīre, advēnī, adventum – arrive
    reveniō, revenīre, revēnī, reventum – come back
    similarly: circumveniō (surround); conveniō (come together, meet);
          inveniō (come upon, find); perveniō (reach); subveniō (come
          to help), etc.

4c   aperiō, aperīre, aperuī, apertum – open
saliō, salīre, saluī – jump
    dēsiliō, dēsilīre, dēsiluī – jump down

4d   sentiō, sentīre, sēnsī, sēnsum – feel
    cōnsentiō, cōnsentīre, cōnsēnsī, cōnsēnsum – agree
    dissentiō, dissentīre, dissēnsī, dissēnsum – disagree

4e   sepeliō, sepelīre, sepelīvī*, sepultum – bury

4f   hauriō, haurīre, hausī, haustum – drain
vinciō, vincīre, vīnxī, vīnctum – bind

4g   *deponent verbs*
mentior, mentīrī, mentītus sum – tell a lie
orior, orīrī, ortus sum – arise

5   *mixed conjugation*

5a   capiō, capere, cēpī, captum – take, capture
    accipiō, accipere, accēpī, acceptum – receive
    suscipiō, suscipere, suscēpī, susceptum – undertake
    similarly: dēcipiō (deceive); incipiō (begin); recipiō (recover), etc.
faciō, facere, fēcī, factum – do
    efficiō, efficere, effēcī, effectum – carry out
    praeficiō, praeficere, praefēcī, praefectum – put in charge
    similarly: afficiō (affect); cōnficiō (finish); interficiō (kill); reficiō (repair),
          etc.
fugiō, fugere, fūgī – flee, run away
    effugiō, effugere, effūgī – escape
iaciō, iacere, iēcī, iactum – throw
    abiciō, abicere, abiēcī, abiectum – throw away
    dēiciō, dēicere, dēiēcī, dēiectum – throw down
    similarly: coniciō (hurl); ēiciō (throw out); iniciō (throw in); reiciō
          (throw back), etc.

---

* sometimes shortened to *audiī, custōdiī, dormiī*, etc.

5b spec, specere, spex, spectum – see*
    circumspici, circumspicere, circumspex, circumspectum – look round
    respici, respicere, respex, respectum – look back
    similarly: aspici (look towards); cnspici (catch sight of); dspici
        (look down); nspici (inspect), etc.

5c cupi, cupere, cupv or cupi, cuptum – desire

5d rapi, rapere, rapu, raptum – seize
    dripi, dripere, dripu, dreptum – tear apart, ransack
    ripi, ripere, ripu, reptum – snatch away

5e *deponent verbs*
    gradior, grad, gressus sum – go
        aggredior, aggred, aggressus sum – advance, attack
        congredior, congred, congressus sum – meet
        similarly: gredior (go out); ingredior (go in);
            prgredior (go forward); regredior (go back), etc.
    morior, mor, mortuus sum – die
    patior, pat, passus sum – suffer

6   *irregular*

6a e, re, i or v, tum (other forms of this verb are listed in **9.1–3**) – go
    exe, exre, exi, exitum – go out
    trnse, trnsre, trnsi, trnsitum – cross
    similarly: abe (go away); ade (go towards); circume (go round);
        pere (perish); rede (return), etc.

6b fer, ferre, tul, ltum (other forms in **9.1–3** and **9.5**) – bring
    affer, afferre, attul, alltum† – bring along
    aufer, auferre, abstul, abltum – take away, steal
    effer, efferre, extul, ltum – bring out
    refer, referre, rettul, reltum – bring back
    similarly: circumfer (carry round); nfer (bring in); offer (offer), etc.

6c f, fier, factus sum (other forms in **9.1–4**) – be made, become

6d memin, meminisse (other forms in **9.7**) – remember
    d, disse (other forms in **9.7**) – hate

6e sum, esse, fu (other forms in **9.1–3**) – be
    absum, abesse, fu – be away, be absent
    possum, posse, potu (other forms in **9.1–3**) – be able
    praesum, praeesse, praefu – be in charge
    similarly: adsum (be present); dsum (be missing);
        prsum (be useful); supersum (be left over, survive), etc.

6f toll, tollere, sustul, subltum – raise, remove

6g vol, velle, volu (other forms in **9.1–3**) – want, be willing
    ml, mlle, mlu (other forms in **9.6**) – prefer
    nl, nlle, nlu (other forms in **9.6**) – not want, refuse

---

* *speci* itself is a fairly rare verb; but the compound verbs *circumspici*, *respici*,
etc. are very common.

†For an explanation of the spelling of these and other forms of compounds of
fer, see **32**.9.

35 Common verbs used with the dative

	literal translation	*natural translation*
tibi appropinquō	I come near to you	I approach you
tibi cōnfīdō	I put trust in you	I trust you
tibi crēdō	I have faith in you	I believe you
tibi displiceō	I am displeasing to you	I displease you
tibi faveō	I show favour to you	I favour you, support you
tibi ignōscō	I am forgiving to you	I forgive you
tibi imperō	I give an order to you	I order you
tibi indulgeō	I am indulgent to you	I indulge you
tibi invideō	I am jealous towards you	I envy you
tibi noceō	I am harmful to you	I hurt you
tibi nūbō	{ *original meaning probably:* I put on the marriage-veil for you }	I (a woman) marry you
tibi obstō	I am an obstacle to you	I get in your way, obstruct you
tibi parcō	I am merciful to you	I spare you
tibi pāreō	I am obedient to you	I obey you
tibi persuādeō	I am persuasive to you	I persuade you
tibi placeō	I am pleasing to you	I please you
tibi resistō	I put up a resistance to you	I resist you
tibi serviō	I am a slave for you	I serve you (as a slave)
tibi studeō	I am devoted to you	I support you, am concerned with you

and many compound verbs, e.g.:

tibi praesum	I am the commander for you	I am in charge of you
tibi subveniō	I come as a rescuer for you	I come to help you

36 Examples of cognate words

(i.e. words related to each other)

1a *verb*

amāre	*to love*
clāmāre	*to shout*
labōrāre	*to work*

1b *noun ending in -or*

amor	*love*
clāmor	*shout*
labor	*work*

2a *adjective*

altus	*high, deep*
magnus	*great*
sōlus	*alone*
fortis	*brave*
multī	*many*

2b *noun ending in -itūdō*

altitūdō	*height, depth*
magnitūdō	*greatness, size*
sōlitūdō	*loneliness, solitude*
fortitūdō	*bravery*
multitūdō	*crowd*

3a *adjective*

amīcus	*friendly*
superbus	*proud, arrogant*
audāx	*bold*
sapiēns	*wise*
trīstis	*sad*

3b *noun ending in -ia*

amīcitia	*friendship*
superbia	*pride, arrogance*
audācia	*boldness*
sapientia	*wisdom*
trīstitia	*sadness*

4a *adjective*

benignus	*kind*
īnfirmus	*weak*
līber	*free*
crūdēlis	*cruel*
gravis	*heavy, serious*

4b *noun ending in -tās*

benignitās	*kindness*
īnfirmitās	*weakness*
lībertās	*freedom*
crūdēlitās	*cruelty*
gravitās	*heaviness, seriousness*

5a *verb (supine shown in brackets)*

arāre (arātum)	*to plough*
spectāre (spectātum)	*to watch*
dūcere (ductum)	*to lead*
vincere (victum)	*to win*

5b *noun ending in -tor*

arātor	*ploughman*
spectātor	*watcher*
ductor	*leader*
victor	*winner*

6a *verb*

nitēre	*to shine*
pallēre	*to be pale*
timēre	*to fear*

6b *noun ending in -or*

nitor	*brightness*
pallor	*paleness*
timor	*fear*

6c *adjective ending in -idus*

nitidus	*bright, shining*
pallidus	*pale*
timidus	*fearful*

7a *verb*

coniūrāre	*to plot, conspire*
haesitāre	*to hesitate*
salūtāre	*to greet*
quaerere	*to search, inquire*
scrībere	*to write*

7b *noun ending in -tiō*

coniūrātiō	*plot, conspiracy*
haesitātiō	*hesitation*
salūtātiō	*greeting*
quaestiō	*inquiry, investigation*
scrīptiō	*writing*

8a *verb*

certāre	*to compete*
fluere	*to flow*
nōmināre	*to name*
impedīre	*to hinder*
vestīre	*to clothe, dress*

8b *noun ending in -men, -mentum*

certāmen	*contest*
flūmen	*river*
nōmen	*name*
impedīmentum	*hindrance*
vestīmentum	*clothing*

9a *verb (supine shown in brackets)*

advenīre (adventum)	*to arrive*
cōnsentīre (cōnsēnsum)	*to agree*
redīre (reditum)	*to return*
monēre (monitum)	*to warn*
plaudere (plausum)	*to applaud*

9b *noun ending in -tus, -sus*

adventus	*arrival*
cōnsēnsus	*agreement*
reditus	*return*
monitus	*warning*
plausus	*applause*

10a *noun*

fōrma	*beauty, appearance*
līmus	*mud*
ōtium	*leisure, idleness*
perīculum	*danger*
pretium	*price, value*

10b *adjective ending in -ōsus*

fōrmōsus	*beautiful*
līmōsus	*muddy*
ōtiōsus	*idle, on holiday*
perīculōsus	*dangerous*
pretiōsus	*precious, valuable*

11a *verb*

aedificāre	*to build*
imperāre	*to order*
gaudēre	*to rejoice, be pleased*
studēre	*to study, be keen on*

11b *noun ending in -ium*

aedificium	*building*
imperium	*power*
gaudium	*joy*
studium	*study, enthusiasm*

12a *verb*

audēre	*to dare*
loquī	*to talk*
mentīrī	*to tell a lie*
pugnāre	*to fight*

12b *adjective ending in -āx*

audāx	*bold, daring*
loquāx	*talkative*
mendāx	*lying, deceitful*
pugnāx	*fond of fighting*

13a *noun*

cēna	*dinner*
culpa	*blame*
lacrima	*tear*
mora	*delay*
pugna	*fight*

13b *verb*

cēnāre	*to dine*
culpāre	*to blame*
lacrimāre	*to weep, cry*
morārī	*to delay*
pugnāre	*to fight*

14a *positive*

scīre	*to know*
volō	*I want*
umquam	*ever*
ōtium	*leisure*

14b *negative*

nescīre	*not to know*
nōlō	*I do not want*
numquam	*never*
negōtium	*non-leisure, i.e. business*

amīcus	*friend*
fēlīx	*lucky*
ūtilis	*useful*

inimīcus	*enemy*
īnfēlīx	*unlucky*
īnūtilis	*useless*

cōnsentīre	*to agree*
facilis	*easy*
similis	*like*

dissentīre	*to disagree*
difficilis	*difficult*
dissimilis	*unlike*

15a *noun*

homō	*man*
liber	*book*
servus	*slave*
cēna	*dinner*
vīlla	*country-house*

15b *diminutive*

homunculus	*little man*
libellus	*little book*
servulus	*little slave*
cēnula	*little dinner*
vīllula	*little country-house*

16a *masculine noun*

deus	*god*
dominus	*master*
fīlius	*son*
saltātor	*dancer (male)*
victor	*winner (male)*

16b *feminine noun*

dea	*goddess*
domina	*mistress*
fīlia	*daughter*
saltātrīx	*dancer (female)*
victrīx	*winner (female)*

For further examples of cognate words, see the list of adjectives and adverbs in **3** and the examples of compound verbs in **34**.

VOCABULARY

The following vocabulary list contains all the words used in the 'further examples' and exercises in this Grammar. They are listed in the ways described in **32**.

a

ā, ab + *abl.* – from; by
abeō, abīre, abiī, abitum – go away
accipiō, accipere, accēpī, acceptum – accept, receive
ad + *acc.* – to, at
adeō – so much, so greatly
adhūc – up till now, still
adipīscor, adipīscī, adeptus sum – receive, obtain
adiuvō, adiuvāre, adiūvī, adiūtum – help
adstō, adstāre, adstitī – stand by
adveniō, advenīre, advēnī, adventum – arrive
aedificō, aedificāre, aedificāvī, aedificātum – build
aeger, aegra, aegrum – sick, ill
Aegyptius, Aegyptia, Aegyptium – Egyptian
afferō, afferre, attulī, adlātum (*sometimes* allātum) – bring
afflīgō, afflīgere, afflīxī, afflīctum – afflict, strike
ager, agrī, m. – field
aggredior, aggredī, aggressus sum – attack
agnus, agnī, m. – lamb
agō, agere, ēgī, āctum – do, act
  grātiās agō – thank, give thanks
agricola, agricolae, m. – farmer
alius, alia, aliud – other, another
  aliī . . . aliī – some . . . others
alter, altera, alterum – the other, another
  alter . . . alter – one . . . the other
ambulō, ambulāre, ambulāvī, ambulātum – walk
amīcus, amīcī, m. – friend
āmittō, āmittere, āmīsī, āmissum – lose
amō, amāre, amāvī, amātum – love, like
amphitheātrum, amphitheātrī, n. – amphitheatre
an – or
  utrum . . . an – whether . . . or
ancilla, ancillae, f. – slave-girl, maid

animal, animālis, n. – animal
annus, annī, m. – year
ante + *acc.* – before
aperiō, aperīre, aperuī, apertum – open
apodytērium, apodytēriī, n. – changing room
appāreō, appārēre, appāruī, appāritum – appear
appropinquō, appropinquāre, appropinquāvī, appropinquātum + *dat.* – approach, come near to
aqua, aquae, f. – water
āra, ārae, f. – altar
arcessō, arcessere, arcessīvī, arcessītum – summon, send for
ardeō, ardēre, arsī – burn, be on fire
ars, artis, f. – art, skill
Athēnae, Athēnārum, f.pl. – Athens
āthlēta, āthlētae, m. – athlete
attonitus, attonita, attonitum – astonished
attulī *see* afferō
auctor, auctōris, m. – creator, originator
audeō, audēre, ausus sum – dare
audiō, audīre, audīvī, audītum – hear
auferō, auferre, abstulī, ablātum – take away, steal
aula, aulae, f. – palace
aurum, aurī, n. – gold
autem – but
auxilium, auxiliī, n. – help
avārus, avārī, m. – miser
avis, avis, f. – bird

b

bellum, bellī, n. – war
  bellum gerō – wage war, campaign
bene – well
benignus, benigna, benignum – kind
bibō, bibere, bibī – drink
bonus, bona, bonum – good
Britannī, Britannōrum, m.pl. – Britons
Britannia, Britanniae, f. – Britain

c

caelum, caelī, n. – sky, heaven

calidus, calida, calidum – hot

callidus, callida, callidum – clever, cunning

candidātus, candidātī, m. – candidate

canis, canis, m. – dog

cantō, cantāre, cantāvī, cantātum – sing

capiō, capere, cēpī, captum – take, catch, capture

captīvus, captīvī, m. – prisoner, captive

caput, capitis, n. – head

carcer, carceris, m. – prison

castra, castrōrum, n.pl. – camp

catēna, catēnae, f. – chain

caveō, cavēre, cāvī, cautum – beware

celebrō, celebrāre, celebrāvī, celebrātum – celebrate

celeriter – quickly, fast

cēlō, cēlāre, cēlāvī, cēlātum – hide

cēna, cēnae, f. – dinner

centum – hundred

centuriō, centuriōnis, m. – centurion

cēterī, cēterae, cētera – the others, the rest

chorus, chorī, m. – chorus, choir

cibus, cibī, m. – food

circumspectō, circumspectāre, circumspectāvī, circumspectātum – look round

circumveniō, circumvenīre, circumvēnī, circumventum – surround

cīvis, cīvis, m.f. – citizen

clāmō, clāmāre, clāmāvī, clāmātum – shout

clāmor, clāmōris, m. – shout, uproar

claudō, claudere, clausī, clausum – shut, close

cliēns, clientis, m. – client

cōgitō, cōgitāre, cōgitāvī, cōgitātum – think, consider

cognōscō, cognōscere, cognōvī, cognitum – get to know, find out

cōgō, cōgere, coēgī, coāctum – force, compel

comitor, comitārī, comitātus sum – accompany

comparō, comparāre, comparāvī, comparātum – obtain

compleō, complēre, complēvī, complētum – fill

conclāve, conclāvis, n. – room

condūcō, condūcere, condūxī, conductum – hire

cōnfīdō, cōnfīdere, cōnfīsus sum + dat. – trust, put trust

cōnor, cōnārī, cōnātus sum – try

cōnsilium, cōnsiliī, n. – plan, idea

cōnsistō, cōnsistere, cōnstitī – stand firm, halt

cōnspiciō, cōnspicere, cōnspexī, cōnspectum – catch sight of

cōnspicor, cōnspicārī, cōnspicātus sum – catch sight of

cōnsul, cōnsulis, m. – consul (senior magistrate)

cōnsūmō, cōnsūmere, cōnsūmpsī, cōnsūmptum – eat, consume

contendō, contendere, contendī, contentum – hurry

contentus, contenta, contentum – satisfied

contrā + acc. – against

coquus, coquī, m. – cook

corpus, corporis, n. – body

cotīdiē – every day

crās – tomorrow

crēdō, crēdere, crēdidī, crēditum + dat. – trust, believe

crūdēlitās, crūdēlitātis, f. – cruelty

cubiculum, cubiculī, n. – bedroom

cuius see quī

cum – when

cūr? – why?

currō, currere, cucurrī, cursum – run

custōs, custōdis, m. – guard

d

dabam see dō

damnō, damnāre, damnāvī, damnātum – condemn

dē + abl. – from, down from; about, over

dea, deae, f. – goddess

dēbeō, dēbēre, dēbuī, dēbitum – ought, should, must

decem – ten

decet, decēre, decuit – is proper
mē decet – I ought

dēcidō, dēcidere, dēcidī – fall down

dēcipiō, dēcipere, dēcēpī, dēceptum – deceive, trick

dedī see dō

deinde – then

dēlectō, dēlectāre, dēlectāvī, dēlectātum – delight, please

dēleō, dēlēre, dēlēvī, dēlētum – destroy

dēnārius, dēnāriī, m. – denarius (a coin)

dēns, dentis, m. – tooth

dērīdeō, dērīdēre, dērīsī, dērīsum – mock, jeer at

dēserō, dēserere, dēseruī, dēsertum –
   desert, leave behind
dēsiliō, dēsilīre, dēsiluī, dēsultum – jump
   down
dēsinō, dēsinere, dēsiī, dēsitum – end,
   cease
dēspērō, dēspērāre, dēspērāvī, dēspērātum
   – despair, give up
deus, deī, m. – god
Dēva, Dēvae, f. – Chester
dīcō, dīcere, dīxī, dictum – say
dictō, dictāre, dictāvī, dictātum – dictate
diēs, diēī, m. f. – day
   diēs nātālis, diēī nātālis, m. – birthday
difficilis, difficile – difficult
dignus, digna, dignum + *abl.* – worthy
dīligenter – carefully
discēdō, discēdere, discessī, discessum –
   depart
discō, discere, didicī – learn
dissimilis, dissimile + *dat.* – dissimilar,
   unlike
diū – for a long time
dīves, *gen.* dīvitis – rich
dīvitiae, dīvitiārum, f.pl. – riches
dō, dare, dedī, datum – give
doceō, docēre, docuī, doctum – teach
domina, dominae, f. – mistress
dominus, dominī, m. – master
domus, domūs, f. – home, house
dōnec – until
dōnum, dōnī, n. – present, gift
dormiō, dormīre, dormīvī, dormītum –
   sleep
dūcō, dūcere, dūxī, ductum – lead
dum – while
duo, duae, duo – two
dux, ducis, m. – leader

e

ē, ex + *abl.* – from, out of
eam *see* is
eandem *see* īdem
eās *see* is
ecce! – see! look!
efficiō, efficere, effēcī, effectum – carry out,
   accomplish
effugiō, effugere, effūgī – escape
effundō, effundere, effūdī, effūsum – pour
   out
ēgī *see* agō
ego, meī – I, me

ēgredior, ēgredī, ēgressus sum – go out
ēheu! – alas!
eī *see* is
eīdem *see* īdem
eīs *see* is
elephantus, elephantī, m. – elephant
ēligō, ēligere, ēlēgī, ēlēctum – choose
emō, emere, ēmī, ēmptum – buy
eō, īre, iī, itum – go
   obviam eō – meet, go to meet
eōdem *see* īdem
epistula, epistulae, f. – letter
eques, equitis, m. – horseman
equus, equī, m. – horse
eram *see* sum
ēripiō, ēripere, ēripuī, ēreptum – snatch
   away
erō *see* sum
es, est *see* sum
et – and
etiam – even, also
eum *see* is
ex, ē + *abl.* – from, out of
excitō, excitāre, excitāvī, excitātum – arouse,
   wake up
exclāmō, exclāmāre, exclāmāvī, exclāmātum
   – exclaim, shout
exeō, exīre, exiī, exitum – go out
exerceō, exercēre, exercuī, exercitum –
   exercise, practise, train
exiguus, exigua, exiguum – small, short
exspectō, exspectāre, exspectāvī,
   exspectātum – wait for
exstinguō, exstinguere, exstīnxī, exstīnctum
   – extinguish, put out
extrā + *acc.* – outside
extrahō, extrahere, extrāxī, extractum – pull
   out

f

faber, fabrī, m. – craftsman
facile – easily
facilis, facile – easy
faciō, facere, fēcī, factum – make, do
   iter faciō – make a journey, travel
   rebelliōnem faciō – rebel
falsus, falsa, falsum – false, untrue
faveō, favēre, fāvī, fautum + *dat.* – favour,
   support
fēmina, fēminae, f. – woman
fenestra, fenestrae, f. – window

ferō, ferre, tulī, lātum – bring, carry
fervidus, fervida, fervidum – intense, fierce
fessus, fessa, fessum – tired
festīnō, festīnāre, festīnāvī, festīnātum – hurry
fidēliter – faithfully
fidēs, fideī, f. – faith
fīlius, fīliī, m. – son
fīō, fierī, factus sum – be made, be done, become
flamma, flammae, f. – flame
flūmen, flūminis, n. – river
foedus, foeda, foedum – foul, horrible
fortis, forte – brave
forum, forī, n. – forum, market-place
fossa, fossae, f. – ditch
frangō, frangere, frēgī, frāctum – break
frāter, frātris, m. – brother
fraus, fraudis, f. – trick
frūmentum, frūmentī, n. – grain
frūstrā – in vain
fugiō, fugere, fūgī, fugitum – run away, flee (from)
fuī see sum
fundus, fundī, m. – farm
fūr, fūris, m. – thief

g

Gallia, Galliae, f. – Gaul
gaudeō, gaudēre, gāvīsus sum – be pleased, rejoice, be delighted
gemma, gemmae, f. – jewel, gem
gener, generī, m. – son-in-law
gerō, gerere, gessī, gestum – achieve
  bellum gerō – wage war, campaign
gladiātor, gladiātōris, m. – gladiator
gladius, gladiī, m. – sword
glōria, glōriae, f. – glory
gracilis, gracile – slender, slim
gradior, gradī, gressus sum – go
Graecus, Graeca, Graecum – Greek
grātiae, grātiārum, f.pl. – thanks
  grātiās agō – thank, give thanks
gustō, gustāre, gustāvī, gustātum – taste

h

habeō, habēre, habuī, habitum – have
habitō, habitāre, habitāvī, habitātum – live
haesitō, haesitāre, haesitāvī, haesitātum – hesitate
haruspex, haruspicis, m. – soothsayer
hasta, hastae, f. – spear

heri – yesterday
hic, haec, hoc – this
Hispānia, Hispāniae, f. – Spain
hodiē – today
homō, hominis, m. – man
hōra, hōrae, f. – hour
horreum, horreī, n. – barn, granary
hortor, hortārī, hortātus sum – encourage, urge
hortus, hortī, m. – garden
hospes, hospitis, m. – guest
hostis, hostis, m.f. – enemy
humilis, humile – low-born, of low class

i

iaciō, iacere, iēcī, iactum – throw
iam – now
iānua, iānuae, f. – door
ībō see eō
id see is
īdem, eadem, idem – (for endings, see 5.6) the same
ignōscō, ignōscere, ignōvī, ignōtum + dat. – forgive
ille, illa, illud – that
immemor, gen. immemoris + gen. – forgetful
impediō, impedīre, impedīvī, impedītum – delay, hinder
imperātor, imperātōris, m. – emperor
imperō, imperāre, imperāvī, imperātum + dat. – order, command
in (1) + acc. – into, onto
in (2) + abl. – in, on
incendō, incendere, incendī, incēnsum – burn, set fire to
incertus, incerta, incertum – uncertain
induō, induere, induī, indūtum – put on
īnferō, īnferre, intulī, inlātum (sometimes illātum) – bring in
ingēns, gen. ingentis – huge
ingredior, ingredī, ingressus sum – enter
inimīcus, inimīcī, m. – enemy
innocēns, gen. innocentis – innocent
inquit – says, said
īnsānus, īnsāna, īnsānum – mad, crazy
īnspiciō, īnspicere, īnspexī, īnspectum – look at, examine
īnstruō, īnstruere, īnstrūxī, īnstrūctum – draw up
interficiō, interficere, interfēcī, interfectum – kill

intrō, intrāre, intrāvī, intrātum – enter
intulī *see* īnferō
inveniō, invenīre, invēnī, inventum – find
invītō, invītāre, invītāvī, invītātum – invite
ipse, ipsa, ipsum – himself, herself, itself
īrātus, īrāta, īrātum – angry
is, ea, id – *(for endings, see* **5**.5) he, she, it
    id quod – what
ita – in this way
Ītalia, Ītaliae, f. – Italy
iter, itineris, n. – journey
    iter faciō – make a journey, travel
iterum – again
iubeō, iubēre, iussī, iussum – order
iūdex, iūdicis, m. – judge
iuvenis, iuvenis, m. – young man

l

labōrō, labōrāre, labōrāvī, labōrātum – work
lacrimō, lacrimāre, lacrimāvī, lacrimātum –
    weep, cry
lapis, lapidis, m. – stone
latrō, latrōnis, m. – robber
lātus *see* ferō
lātus, lāta, lātum – wide
laudō, laudāre, laudāvī, laudātum – praise
laus, laudis, f. – praise, fame
lavō, lavāre, lāvī, lautum – wash
lectus, lectī, m. – couch, bed
lēgātus, lēgātī, m. – commander
legō, legere, lēgī, lēctum – read
leō, leōnis, m. – lion
liber, librī, m. – book
līberō, līberāre, līberāvī, līberātum – free,
    set free
lībertās, lībertātis, f. – freedom
libet, libēre, libuit, libitum – is pleasing
    mihi libet – I am glad
licet, licēre, licuit, licitum – is allowed
    mē licet – I may
līmen, līminis, n. – threshold, doorway
locus, locī, m. – place
Londinium, Londiniī, n. – London
loquor, loquī, locūtus sum – speak
lūdō, lūdere, lūsī, lūsum – play
lupus, lupī, m. – wolf
lūx, lūcis, f. – light, daylight
    prīmā lūce – at dawn
lyricus, lyrica, lyricum – lyric

m

magister, magistrī, m. – master, teacher
magnus, magna, magnum – big, large, great
    maximus, maxima, maximum – very big,
    very great, greatest
malus, mala, malum – evil, bad
    pessimus, pessima, pessimum – very bad,
    worst
māne – in the morning
maneō, manēre, mānsī, mānsum – remain,
    stay
mare, maris, n. – sea
marītus, marītī, m. – husband
māter, mātris, f. – mother
maximus *see* magnus
mē *see* ego
medicus, medicī, m. – doctor
medius, media, medium – middle
membrum, membrī, n. – limb
meminī, meminisse – remember
mendāx, mendācis, m. – liar
mēnsa, mēnsae, f. – table
mēnsis, mēnsis, m. – month
mentior, mentīrī, mentītus sum – lie, tell a
    lie
mercātor, mercātōris, m. – merchant
mereō, merēre, meruī, meritum – deserve
meus, mea, meum – my, mine
mihi *see* ego
mīles, mīlitis, m. – soldier
mīlitō, mīlitāre, mīlitāvī, mīlitātum – be a
    soldier
minus – less
mīrābilis, mīrābile – marvellous, strange
mīror, mīrārī, mīrātus sum – admire,
    wonder at
miser, misera, miserum – miserable,
    wretched, sad
mittō, mittere, mīsī, missum – send
modus, modī, m. – manner, way, kind
    quō modō? – how? in what way?
moneō, monēre, monuī, monitum – warn,
    advise
mōns, montis, m. – mountain
morbus, morbī, m. – illness
morior, morī, mortuus sum – die
moritūrus, moritūra, moritūrum – about to
    die, going to die
mox – soon
multō – much
multus, multa, multum – much
mūrus, mūrī, m. – wall

n

nam – for

nārrō, nārrāre, nārrāvī, nārrātum – tell, relate

(diēs) nātālis, (diēī) nātālis, m. – birthday

nauta, nautae, m. – sailor

nāvis, nāvis, f. – ship

-ne – *asks a question*

nē – that . . . not, so that . . . not, in order that . . . not

necō, necāre, necāvī, necātum – kill

negō, negāre, negāvī, negātum – deny, say that . . . not

nēmō – no one, nobody

nescio, nescīre, nescīvī, nescītum – not know

nihil – nothing

nimis – too much, too

nisi – unless, if . . . not

noceō, nocēre, nocuī, nocitum + *dat.* – hurt

nōlō, nōlle, nōluī – not want, refuse
  nōlī, nōlīte – do not, don't

nōmen, nōminis, n. – name

nōn – not

nōnne? – surely?

nōs – we, us

noster, nostra, nostrum – our

novus, nova, novum – new

nox, noctis, f. – night

nūllus, nūlla, nūllum – not any, no

num? – surely . . . not?

numerō, numerāre, numerāvī, numerātum – count

nunc – now

nūntiō, nūntiāre, nūntiāvī, nūntiātum – announce

nūntius, nūntiī, m. – messenger

o

obscēnus, obscēna, obscēnum – rude, obscene

obscūrus, obscūra, obscūrum – dark, gloomy

obtineō, obtinēre, obtinuī, obtentum – occupy

obviam eō, obviam īre, obviam iī, obviam itum + *dat.* – meet, go to meet

occāsiō, occāsiōnis, f. – opportunity

occīdō, occīdere, occīdī, occīsum – kill

occupō, occupāre, occupāvī, occupātum – seize, take over

octō – eight

ōdī, ōdisse – hate, dislike

odium, odiī, n. – hatred
  odiō sum – be hateful

offerō, offerre, obtulī, oblātum – offer

ōmen, ōminis, n. – omen

omnis, omne – all, every
  omnia – all, everything

opera, operae, f. – work, attention

oportet, oportēre, oportuit – is right
  mē oportet – I must

oppidum, oppidī, n. – town

opprimō, opprimere, oppressī, oppressum – crush

p

paenitet, paenitēre, paenituit – causes regret
  mē paenitet – I regret, I am sorry

parcō, parcere, pepercī, parsum + *dat.* – spare

parēns, parentis, m.f. – parent

pāreō, pārēre, pāruī, pāritum + *dat.* – obey

pāstor, pāstōris, m. – shepherd

pater, patris, m. – father

patior, patī, passus sum – suffer, endure, allow

pauper, *gen.* pauperis – poor

pecūnia, pecūniae, f. – money

pepercī *see* parcō

per +*acc.* – through, along

pereō, perīre, periī, peritum – die, perish

perficiō, perficere, perfēcī, perfectum – finish

perīculōsus, perīculōsa, perīculōsum – dangerous

perīculum, perīculī, n. – danger

persuādeō, persuādēre, persuāsī, persuāsum + *dat.* – persuade

perterritus, perterrita, perterritum – terrified

perveniō, pervenīre, pervēnī, perventum – reach, arrive at

pessimus *see* malus

petō, petere, petīvī, petītum – seek, beg for, ask for

pictūra, pictūrae, f. – picture

piscis, piscis, m. – fish

placeō, placēre, placuī, placitum + *dat.* – please, suit

plaudō, plaudere, plausī, plausum – applaud, clap

pluit, pluere, pluit – rain

poēta, poētae, m. – poet
polliceor, pollicērī, pollicitus sum – promise
pompa, pompae, f. – procession
Pompēiī, Pompēiōrum, m.pl. – Pompeii
pōnō, pōnere, posuī, positum – put, place
pōns, pontis, m. – bridge
populus, populī, m. – people
porcus, porcī, m. – pig
porta, portae, f. – gate
portō, portāre, portāvī, portātum – carry
portus, portūs, m. – harbour
possum, posse, potuī – can, be able
postquam – after, when
postulō, postulāre, postulāvī, postulātum –
    demand
praecō, praecōnis, m. – herald
praemium, praemiī, n. – prize, reward
praesum, praeesse, praefuī + dat. – be in
    charge of
praetereō, praeterīre, praeteriī, praeteritum
    – pass by, go past
precor, precārī, precātus sum – pray
pretiōsus, pretiōsa, pretiōsum – expensive,
    precious
prīmus, prīma, prīmum – first
    prīmā lūce – at dawn
prīncipia, prīncipiōrum, n.pl. –
    headquarters
priusquam – before
prōcēdō, prōcēdere, prōcessī, prōcessum –
    advance, proceed
proficīscor, proficīscī, profectus sum – set
    out
prōgredior, prōgredī, prōgressus sum –
    advance
prohibeō, prohibēre, prohibuī, prohibitum –
    prevent
prōmittō, prōmittere, prōmīsī, prōmissum –
    promise
prope + acc. – near
prūdēns, gen. prūdentis – shrewd, sensible
pudet, pudēre, puduit, puditum – causes
    shame
    mē pudet – I am ashamed
puella, puellae, f. – girl
puer, puerī, m. – boy
pugna, pugnae, f. – fight
pugnō, pugnāre, pugnāvī, pugnātum –
    fight
pūniō, pūnīre, pūnīvī, pūnītum – punish
puto, putāre, putāvī, putātum – think

q

quam – how
    tam . . . quam – as . . . as
quamquam – although
quamvīs – although
quandō? – when?
quārē? – why?
quasi – as if
-que – and
quī, quae, quod – (for endings, see 5.7) who,
    which
    id quod – what
quia – because
quīdam, quaedam, quoddam – one, a
    certain
quīntus, quīnta, quīntum – fifth
quis? quid? – who? what?
quō modō? – how? in what way?
quod – because
quot? – how many?

r

rapiō, rapere, rapuī, raptum – seize, grab
rebelliō, rebelliōnis, f. – rebellion, uprising
    rebelliōnem faciō – rebel
recipiō, recipere, recēpī, receptum –
    recover, take back
recitō, recitāre, recitāvī, recitātum – recite,
    read out
recūsō, recūsāre, recūsāvī, recūsātum –
    refuse
reddō, reddere, reddidī, redditum – give
    back
redeō, redīre, rediī, reditum – return, go
    back, come back
redūcō, redūcere, redūxī, reductum – lead
    back
reficiō, reficere, refēcī, refectum – repair
rēgīna, rēgīnae, f. – queen
regiō, regiōnis, f. – region
regredior, regredī, regressus sum – go back,
    return
relinquō, relinquere, relīquī, relictum –
    leave
rēs, reī, f. – thing, business
resistō, resistere, restitī + dat. – resist
respondeō, respondēre, respondī,
    respōnsum – reply
retineō, retinēre, retinuī, retentum – keep,
    restrain
reveniō, revenīre, revēnī, reventum – come
    back, return

rēx, rēgis, m. – king
rīdeō, rīdēre, rīsī, rīsum – laugh, smile
rīpa, rīpae, f. – river bank
rogō, rogāre, rogāvī, rogātum – ask
Rōma, Rōmae, f. – Rome
Rōmānī, Rōmānōrum, m.pl. – Romans
ruō, ruere, ruī – rush
rūs, rūris, n. – country, countryside

s

sacerdōs, sacerdōtis, m. – priest
sacrificō, sacrificāre, sacrificāvī, sacrificātum
   – sacrifice
saepe – often
saeviō, saevīre, saeviī, saevītum – be in a
   rage
saevus, saeva, saevum – savage, cruel
salūtō, salūtāre, salūtāvī, salūtātum – greet,
   hail
satis – enough
scelestus, scelesta, scelestum – wicked
scelus, sceleris, n. – crime
scindō, scindere, scidī, scissum – tear, cut
scio, scīre, scīvī, scītum – know
scrībō, scrībere, scrīpsī, scrīptum – write
sē – himself, herself, themselves
   (for se *used in indirect statements, see* **25**.4d)
secundus, secunda, secundum – second
sedeō, sedēre, sēdī, sessum – sit
semper – always
senātor, senātōris, m. – senator
senex, senis, m. – old man
septem – seven
sequor, sequī, secūtus sum – follow
serviō, servīre, servīvī, servītum + *dat*. –
   serve (as a slave)
servō, servāre, servāvī, servātum – save,
   look after
servus, servī, m. – slave
sevērē – severely
sexāgintā – sixty
sextus, sexta, sextum – sixth
sī – if
Sicilia, Siciliae, f. – Sicily
sīcut – like
signum, signī, n. – sign, signal
silva, silvae, f. – wood
sim *see* sum
similis, simile + *dat*. – similar
simulac, simulatque – as soon as
soleō, solēre, solitus sum – be accustomed

sollicitus, sollicita, sollicitum – worried,
   anxious
sonō, sonāre, sonuī, sonitum – sound
soror, sorōris, f. – sister
spectātor, spectātōris, m. – spectator
spectō, spectāre, spectāvī, spectātum – look
   at, watch
spērō, spērāre, spērāvī, spērātum – hope,
   expect
statim – at once
statua, statuae, f. – statue
stō, stāre, stetī, statum – stand
strepitus, strepitūs, m. – noise, din
stultus, stulta, stultum – stupid, foolish
suāviter – sweetly
sub + *abl*. – under, beneath
subitō – suddenly
sum, esse, fuī – be
summus, summa, summum – highest,
   greatest
superbē – arrogantly, proudly
superō, superāre, superāvī, superātum –
   overcome, surpass
supplicium, suppliciī, n. – punishment,
   penalty
surgō, surgere, surrēxī, surrēctum – get up,
   rise
suspicor, suspicārī, suspicātus sum –
   suspect
suus, sua, suum – his, her, their

t

taberna, tabernae, f. – shop, inn
taceō, tacēre, tacuī, tacitum – be silent, be
   quiet
tacitus, tacita, tacitum – quiet, silent, in
   silence
tam – so
   tam . . . quam – as . . . as
tamen – however
tandem – at last
tangō, tangere, tetigī, tāctum – touch
tantus, tanta, tantum – so great, such a great
tardus, tarda, tardum – late, slow
taurus, taurī, m. – bull
tē *see* tū
tempestās, tempestātis, f. – storm
templum, templī, n. – temple
temptō, temptāre, temptāvī, temptātum –
   try, put to the test
tempus, temporis, n. – time

terribilis, terribile – terrible
testis, testis, m.f. – witness
theātrum, theātrī, n. – theatre
timeō, timēre, timuī – be afraid, fear
tot – so many
tōtus, tōta, tōtum – whole
trādō, trādere, trādidī, trāditum – hand over
trahō, trahere, trāxī, tractum – drag, draw
trānseō, trānsīre, trānsiī, trānsitum – cross
trēs, tria – three
tū, tuī – you (singular)
tuba, tubae, f. – trumpet
tulī *see* ferō
tūtus, tūta, tūtum – safe
tuus, tua, tuum – your (singular), yours

u

ubi – where, when
ultimus, ultima, ultimum – last
umbra, umbrae, f. – shadow, ghost
umquam – ever
unda, undae, f. – wave
undique – on all sides
urbs, urbis, f. – city
ut – (1) as
ut – (2) that, so that, in order that
utinam – if only, I wish that
ūtor, ūtī, ūsus sum + *abl.* – use
utrum – whether
    utrum . . . an – whether . . . or

v

valdē – very much, very
vehementer – violently, loudly
vehō, vehere, vexī, vectum – carry
vellem *see* volō
vēndō, vēndere, vēndidī, vēnditum – sell
venēnum, venēnī, n. – poison
venia, veniae, f. – mercy
veniō, venīre, vēnī, ventum – come
verbum, verbī, n. – word
vereor, verērī, veritus sum – be afraid, fear
vērum, vērī, n. – truth
vester, vestra, vestrum – your (plural)
vestīmenta, vestīmentōrum, n.pl. – clothes
vetō, vetāre, vetuī, vetitum – forbid
vexō, vexāre, vexāvī, vexātum – annoy
via, viae, f. – street
victima, victimae, f. – victim
victor, victōris, m. – victor, winner
videō, vidēre, vīdī, vīsum – see

vīlla, vīllae, f. – country-house, villa
vinciō, vincīre, vīnxī, vīnctum – bind, tie up
vincō, vincere, vīcī, victum – conquer, win,
    be victorious
vīnum, vīnī, n. – wine
vir, virī, m. – man
virgō, virginis, f. – virgin
vīsitō, vīsitāre, vīsitāvī, vīsitātum – visit
vīta, vītae, f. – life
vītō, vītāre, vītāvī, vītātum – avoid
vituperō, vituperāre, vituperāvī,
    vituperātum – blame, curse
vīvō, vīvere, vīxī, victum – live
vocō, vocāre, vocāvī, vocātum – call
volō, velle, voluī – want
volō, volāre, volāvī, volātum – fly
vōs – you (plural)
vulnerō, vulnerāre, vulnerāvī, vulnerātum –
    wound, injure
vulnus, vulneris, n. – wound

INDEX

In this index, the bold numbers refer to Sections, followed by paragraph numbers. So, for example, the Accusative of time will be found in Section **14**, paragraph 3b, and Section **15**, paragraph 1a.